TIES ACROSS TIME

TIES ACROSS TIME:
A MEMOIR

A Woman's Life In Social Work

by
Merle Updike Davis

CREATIVE ARTS BOOK COMPANY
Berkeley • California

Ties Across Time is published by Donald S. Ellis
and distributed by Creative Arts Book Company

For information contact:
Creative Arts Book Company
833 Bancroft Way
Berkeley, California 94710
1-800-848-7789

ISBN 0-88739-366-7
Library of Congress Catalog Number 2001095294
Printed in the United States of America

This book is dedicated to the social workers of the twentieth century and to those who will follow them in the next century.

CONTENTS

Acknowledgements

It's not easy to describe my deep feelings of appreciation for those who inspired me to write this book–family members, friends, teachers, students, clients and colleagues. I am indebted to the following individuals for their encouragement and help which made it possible for me to complete it:

Robert Cullers, my cousin, who is a journalist and editor, for his belief in my story and his counsel.

Peggy Newgarden, Ph.D. in Public Administration for her optimism that it was a book that needed to be published, and her persistent reminder that it was my book, no matter what direction others suggested. It was she who pushed me to find its structure, and who, with the help of Rachel Levin, her assistant, translated my handwritten manuscript into a first draft.

Emily Hancock, Ph.D., author of *The Girl Within* and editor of *Moxie* magazine, who critiqued the book proposal and suggested the title.

Elise Blumenfeld, Ph.D., Clinical Social Worker, and my friend, who helped me find my voice again after a labored re-write and edited my adaptation of the book for the Rosemary Lukton Memorial Lecture delivered at the

California Institute for Clinical Social Work in May 1999.

I would like thank those who read the first draft of the book for their comments and suggestions. I particularly appreciate the questions from members of the younger generations who wanted to know how my experience of historical events such as, the Depression, World War II and the 60s shaped my life and my passion for my work. In addition, I want to thank the members of two clinical social worker study groups, my writing group, the WIN-WIN William Saroyan Writer's Conference, the Northbrae Community Church and the California Institute for Clinical Social Work for hearing me out.

I am grateful to Don Ellis, publisher, Paul Samuelson, editor, and the staff of Creative Arts Book Company for making this book a reality.

And finally, I want to acknowledge the contribution of my husband, Robert L. Davis, whose love and support made the difference in my life, my work, and in this book. His balancing act of staying out of the way, and being available, is deeply appreciated. Without his patient and untiring efforts the book would never have been completed. He reproduced on the computer however many copies of the handwritten manuscript I put before him and helped to keep me focused.

Preface

*"My mouth shall speak of wisdom; and the meditation
of my heart shall be of understanding."*
Psalms 49:3

This book is a memoir of my life in social work. Life in
work; work in life. They belong together as a part of the whole
person principle of social work—body, mind, and spirit—and
of the whole person I have tried to become.

As I ended my career as a Licensed Clinical Social Worker
in 1996, I found myself confronting a massive assault on the
human values and human services I had spent my life uphold-
ing. Political threats were made in the U.S. Congress that welfare must be replaced by philanthropy, that orphanages would
need to be reopened for the care of dependent and neglected
children. President Clinton signed the Welfare Reform Act
into law on August 22, 1996, setting adrift thirteen million
people including eight million children. Social Security and
Medicare were in jeopardy.

Whenever I walked down the street in my home community in Berkeley, California, an affluent city in a thriving economy, I was greeted by homeless and hungry people, some of whom were mentally ill. The safety net for disadvantaged people was disappearing.

When I made the choice to retire, I looked forward to enjoying art, music, travel, and being a grandparent. I told myself I would volunteer for the symphony instead of social service organizations.

How could I enjoy the creative pursuits I had envisioned for this stage of my life when I felt so fired up about the dark vision that clouded the political future? My plans for a tranquil retirement no longer seemed relevant.

Plans were under way to celebrate the centennial of professional social work in the United States in 1998. Columbia University School of Social Work had offered the first formal training courses in 1898 and would set the celebration in motion. I am a graduate of that school and have spent more than half the century and most of my life as a social work practitioner in child welfare, mental health, and in private practice.

Josephine Nieves, M.S.W., Ph.D., Executive Director of the National Association of Social Workers, challenged social workers "to use every opportunity to inform and transform public opinion because social workers are America's heroes" in a May 1997 editorial in the *National Association of Social Workers News.*

The public has many erroneous notions about social workers, about their training, about what they do. As paradoxical as it may seem, at the same time this nation moves into welfare reform, the need for social workers is increasing. For the past several years, *U.S. News and World Report* has listed social work as one of the twenty-five best jobs of the future. In the United States, social workers provide more mental health services than any other profession.

The necessity to chronicle the story of my life and work as a part of the history of social work proclaimed itself. It was time to speak out, to stand up and be counted. I wanted to tell the story of my personal and professional journey to inspire others to continue with the challenge.

How could I paint a picture of the contribution of practicing social workers in the first century of social work in the United States that could be dusted off, rediscovered, and again used in the next century? Social workers are as uniquely different as the persons they work with. Still, I felt that my story was representative of the course taken by thousands of practicing social workers in the last century, that it furnished a bridge from the past and to the future.

My challenge was to portray the social worker as a compassionate human being who has broad and diverse experience in work and in life. One with a head and a heart.

The narrative has taken the form of a chronological journey. The complexity of my identity as a social worker is matched by the intricate facets of my identity as a woman of the twentieth century. The lines of my personal development and my professional development sometimes ran a parallel course but often intertwined. My search for connection and affiliation is one of the underlying themes.

I am not a theoretician. My focus has been on doing, not theorizing. Yet, I think it is important to understand one's own history in order to bring to bear upon one's work the totality of personal and professional experience.

In telling this story in the context of the twentieth century, the historical development of social work can no more be left out than some of the major historical events of the century. This history is still evolving, and is one of the reasons I wrote the book.

My life and work is described as I remember and interpret it from the now perspective of the clinical social worker and the whole person I have become. That viewpoint is, of course, affected by the vagaries of recollection and the nuances of meaning I have attached to it in the writing of the story.

I once heard it said that the integrity of a memoir depends upon what is left out as well as what is included. There are many intentional omissions in this book. Whenever I have included case examples as illustrative material, all names, identifying characteristics, and other details have been changed. The names and identities of some persons in my social and romantic experiences have also been changed.

I trust that social workers at the beginning, middle, and end of their careers will laugh and cry as they trace their own lives, and walk my path with me. I hope that they, and casual readers alike, will find something to identify with in the search for self-understanding. I anticipate that women of today will find lessons in my adventurous, exciting, and rewarding journey. Most of all, I hope all readers will find a message that leads them to become more involved in the public dialogue concerning services and material necessities for those who are left out, and the growing division in our society between the haves and the have-nots.

TIES ACROSS TIME

Merle Louise Updike, age 3—over the stile and the rail fence, on her way to Hattie's house on the neighboring farm near Orlean, Virginia

I. PREPARATION

Growing Up In Fauquier County

1923-1944

Chapter 1:

ISOLATION-CONNECTION

As a child of three, I wandered barefoot through the edge of the woods, waded a stream, climbed a rail fence, and crossed a field filled with grazing cattle, to Hattie's house; she was outside working in her garden. I left my handprints in the rising dough on her kitchen table. Hattie had been my live-in caretaker while my mother taught school until I was two. She let me walk barefoot through the snow to toughen me up so cockleburs wouldn't hurt bare feet.

That daring and courageous search to find Hattie represents my earliest effort to break through the personal and social isolation I experienced as a little child. I wanted a reaction, a response to those handprints I left in the rising dough.

Looking back, searching out, understanding what I am, where I am—the source and the derivation—has been a continuous process for me. Social workers join with the sages of the past in knowing that to understand others we must first understand ourselves.

I grew up on a farm in the foothills of the Blue Ridge

Mountains in Fauquier County, Virginia. Living on that farm, in an impoverished rural community during the Depression, provided the basic preparation for my life and for my career as a social worker. The experience put me in touch with my internal psyche and sent me on a life-long search for connection. My infantile hunger for personal contact grew to include a yearning for interpersonal interaction with others. Living on a farm taught me a closeness with nature, the seasons, the cycles of growth in animal and plant life, a sense of balance between want and plenty. The sensual stimulation of sight, sound, and touch sharpened my powers of observation.

I observed extreme poverty, disease, suffering, accidental injury, death, suicide, and mental illness. My parents provided models of compassion and generosity in confronting such misfortunes. Racial and class differences in a Southern culture, in a community devastated by the Civil War only a few generations before, had enormous impact.

The 350 acre farm, where I was born in 1923, was three miles from Orlean, the nearest village and equidistant, eleven miles, from Warrenton the county seat and Marshall where I finished high school. This acreage, near the Rappahannock River, was carved out of Wheatland and Prospect Hill, a large estate that Chief Justice John Marshall had bought for one of his sons before the Civil War.

The farm was surrounded by woodland. We couldn't see another house. If we heard an automobile, we rushed outside to see who was arriving.

My parents had bought this farm, and moved over the Blue Ridge Mountains from the Shenandoah Valley of Virginia to the Piedmont plateau, in 1922. My father, Rubert Otto Updike (Born 1895), and my mother, Arthelia Cullers (born 1899), were brought up in the same tiny village. Often when they compared the village to the farm, one or the other of them would say, "Law, we thought of Bentonville as a metropolis!" At the turn of the century Bentonville was connected to the outside world by the Norfolk and Western

Railroad, which ran daily passenger service, and by the telephone and telegraph. On the farm, there were no modern conveniences: no indoor plumbing, no electricity.

My brother still owns and operates the farm. To get there today, one still takes a road through a mile of woodland. I knew that woodland in all seasons. I walked through muddy ruts on the same road to catch the school bus. The seasonal changes became a part of me—leaves turning color in the fall, the ice and snow of winter, the fresh green of spring.

Our old farmhouse is gone. It burned down in 1946, and with it all the pictures, artifacts, and mementos of my childhood. But the land looks much the same as it did: rolling hills and pastureland with grazing sheep and cattle, open fields with springs and streams, clearly marked fence rows. The breezes blow on my cheeks from the same direction they blew when I was a child, and I remember the scent of the tulip poplar at the edge of the hay field.

My childhood and youth were secluded by today's standards. Many of my recollections are of an idyllic childhood. Yet, at times, I was aware of my longing for others. I sensed my parents' feelings of isolation. Isolation was the predominant motif of our way of life in the 20s and 30s.

This excerpt from my mother's journal written in her 80s captures her view of her early life in Fauquier County:

> *"Rubert and I had been going together for a couple of years. Even though I loved Rubert and wanted to be with him, I knew my life would be totally different from the way I had been living. He wanted to buy a farm and I agreed.*
>
> *We found the farm in Fauquier County and bought it for $12,000. He had two horses, a wagon and a plow. My mother gave me a bed, a dresser, some blankets, and linens. We bought a cook stove for $5 and we were in business.*
>
> *I was very homesick and lonely as we didn't know*

*anyone. I had never done much house work—washing,
cooking or gardening—so that year was very hard.
Rubert insisted on buying a piano. We bought a big
Steinway-grand, really a beautiful cabinet but tinny
sound. Rubert had his violin. So we had music when
we were not too tired to play it. Wheatley School had
been closed for several years, but there were enough
children around to get it opened and I started teaching
the seven-grade, one-room school in October, a life
saver for my peace of mind, and financially. Even
though the pay was only $70 a month, it seemed like a
fortune. I got pregnant in September and, believe it or
not, we were both too dumb to know what was making me feel so badly.*

*Merle Louise Updike was born on June 20,1923.
Rubert and I were delighted with the baby but green as
grass about how to tend one. I went mostly by a baby
book I had ordered and made many mistakes. Baby
books then said to let a baby cry; to pick up a baby
would spoil the child. I still think about letting Merle
cry in her crib in a cold room and wonder about the
damage it did in her life.*

*In September, I started teaching again. We hired
Hattie and her husband, Henry, who moved into the
kitchen and bedroom over the main kitchen. Henry
worked on the farm and Hattie took care of Merle."*

So there I was, a baby in a cold room on an isolated farm
in Virginia, in the early part of the century. The road from
Fauquier County had many twists and turns. As I look back
on the personal trauma and dreadful conditions of my community in the Depression, I am aware of the multi-deter-
mined motivation for my career as a social worker.

When I was four, a crucial event that informed my life was
the death of my maternal grandmother in an automobile accident, which I narrowly avoided. I was offered the choice of

riding in a car with my grandmother or in another car with Uncle Elbert. I chose to ride with Uncle Elbert because he always had chewing gum. I have no conscious memory of my grandmother, which is strange, because I remember everyone else I knew at that time. She had lived with us and taken care of me after Hattie moved to a neighboring farm.

For years, I told myself I had never dealt with the loss of my grandmother in my psychoanalysis. But, interestingly enough, when I heard of the death of my psychoanalyst twenty-five years later, I experienced, for the first time, a full flood of grief. Before, I had always felt numb in the face of loss. Not until my 60s, in a peer consultation group, did I understand that I had equated loving with losing the loved one. This vignette demonstrates for me how we continue to try throughout the life cycle to integrate early events. I know I am still not finished dealing with this loss.

After many years of speculating about what my early formative years must have been like, I eventually settled for "good enough" mothering, in Winnicott's terms. My first memories are probably screen memories, but they are happy ones that suggest the joy of feeling close to my parents. One is a memory of interaction with my father while he is singing and teaching me to sing "Here we go round the mulberry bush." Snow is on the ground; he is pushing me in a broad shovel with a short handle around and around a bush in our backyard. In another memory, I am watching my mother play the big, old square piano, in the lamplight, while my parents sing "My Blue Heaven," a 20s song. The line, "Just Molly and me and baby makes three," warmly encloses me in their nest.

My family's social contact was extremely limited in those years. My father worked from dawn to dark on the farm. The only time we went to town was when he needed farm supplies. Once a week, on Saturday evening when the farm work was done, he drove us, in the open touring car, to Orlean to get the mail. Once, I asked the postmaster, Mr. Thee Moore, who took us into the post office by kerosene lantern light, to please build a sidewalk because I thought Orlean must surely be a town. It had two country stores, two churches, a mill, a black-smith shop, a school, and ten houses.

My social circle began to expand after my brother, Rubert Otto Updike, Jr., was born March 12, 1927, before my fourth birthday. My mother prepared me for the birth of a baby by telling me about the "stork" and pointed out a large gray heron by our creek as the stork.

I stayed with Sam and Pearl Hall, friends of my parents, for some weeks before my brother's birth and remember cozy baths in a tin tub by their wood stove and walks with Pearl in the fields. I was disappointed the first time I saw my baby brother because I was not allowed to put him in my doll carriage like my baby doll. I couldn't understand why my mother was in bed and no one explained.

My father's brother, Uncle Elbert, married Aunt Linda in the 30s. They bought Riverside, a big farm near ours and, after moving there, started their family, which grew to include nine children. I loved the newborn babies as they arrived and found Aunt Linda's home an attractive, relaxed place to visit. She was very open and casual in explaining where babies came from and the birthing process which was my first education about sex. My mother had sent for books from the Children's Bureau and read me the first one about the birds and the bees. We never got the second book.

Because we saw so few people, Grant Woods' painting, "Threshing Time," captures perfectly for me the air of excitement about the biggest social event of the year. Uncle Elbert would bring his threshing machine to our farm. As many as twenty men and boys from neighboring farms would bring their horses and wagons and join together for the threshing activities. I helped my mother prepare the sumptuous noon-day meal, which, in addition to fried chicken and sugar cured ham and heaping mounds of vegetables, always included hot biscuits, corn bread, and homemade pies.

Socialization was difficult for me throughout grade school

and high school. I was unsure of myself and self-conscious, but tried to conceal it. I observed the manners, appearance, and behavior of my peers. Relatives and teachers seemed to see me as self-assured; I was often asked to perform: sing, dance, recite, and play the piano at family gatherings, and church or school functions. But performing was different from socializing and interacting with other children.

My parents encouraged social contact with my school friends, but our playtime together was limited to a few overnights each year at my home or theirs. I loved staying overnight with my friend, Helen. Her mother's kitchen is still a magical memory. I can see a nickeltrimmed, black iron cook stove dancing with the warmth of the fire; a humming teakettle; the jars of preserves on the window sill; the tin water buckets by the door. Ten of us children sat on wooden benches around her table eating beans, cabbage, and hot biscuits with blackberry jam.

Orlean Methodist Church and its sister-church Wesley Chapel, five miles down the road, near Waterloo were the centers of social activity in our community. Sunday school picnics and ice cream festivals were big events.

When I became an adolescent, I was awarded scholarships to church camps and 4-H club conferences at Virginia Polytechnic Institute. I began to make friends outside the Orlean community. My parents were generous with their hospitality for my friends from town who enjoyed weekends at our home in the country. Once my mother made Brunswick stew in an iron pot over an open fire for a picnic on the Rappahannock River for my friends, who included eight teenagers, boys and girls.

Looking back, I wouldn't trade my early years in the country on the farm for any other part of my lifetime experience. One of the disappointments of my life was that I never returned to live in Fauquier County again. For many years I hoped I might build a home in the Virginia woods overlooking the farm. But I still return there to visit and wander over the hills through the fields and the woodland. My curiosity, imagination, and sense of adventure were developed in that crucible of nature. The stimulation of soft grass on bare feet, the call of the meadow lark, the sight of the ever changing sky as it met the horizon, sharpened my powers of observation. The view of the Blue Ridge Mountains I grew up with became a symbol of stability and permanence. The geography of place became a part of me. Learning to appreciate solitude led to a search for self-understanding that I have needed in my life and in my work. My longing for social contact sent me on a life-long search for connection.

Chapter 2:

SOCIO-ECONOMIC MILIEU
OF THE DEPRESSION

As I review the beginning awareness of my inner life, I am struck by omissions within the social context of my life. For instance, little was said about class distinctions and racial differences in my world, but there were well-established traditions and unspoken assumptions.

The Southern culture set up rigid boundaries. When I went to public school, there were at least four levels of social class among my school peers. These groups included the "poor white trash"; the respectable, hard working poor; the financially, somewhat, better-off middle class, and the often poor but proud "blue bloods" or first families of Virginia. I would have given my heart to be invited to the homes of some of the children I found most attractive. And I knew some other children felt the same way about my home.

This social stratification seemingly had little to do with economics in the Depression era as all of these groups were affected by the same dire economic circumstances.

My parents saw these class distinctions as artificial and tried to teach us to evaluate each person on his or her own merits. But at the same time, they considered themselves as solid middle class. My mother often told us stories of the pride her father, a country physician, had taught her to have in herself and her family. The members of my father's family were very clear that they considered themselves of a higher class than most of their acquaintances. These were confusing messages.

As I look back with a greater appreciation of history than I had in my early years, I think our small-circumscribed Orlean community had never fully recovered from the devastation of the Civil War and the effect of the Reconstruction era. Most of the families I knew had suffered economic deprivation for several generations. The results of the Reconstruction era had become a part of a way of life.

During the Civil War, Andrew "Stonewall" Jackson's Confederate army crossed the Rappahannock River and marched on an old road through our farm to Orlean on their way to the battle of Manassas. The Yankees burned mills and houses near Waterloo less than five miles from our home. The Wesley Chapel church was used as a hospital for men brought from the battle of Manassas and from local skirmishes between the Yankees and the Confederates. Their armies camped across the Rappahannock River from one another.

When I attended church at Wesley Chapel as a small child, my imagination was caught up in stories I heard about slaves helping to build that old stone church in the woods.

I knew an old man and his wife, Uncle Jo and Aunt Betty, who had once been slaves. Whenever my father took me to their home, which was whitewashed, inside and out, and meticulously kept, they entertained me, and gave me some small natural keepsake—a pebble, an acorn, a flower.

A neighborhood of our community was made up of African American homeowners. The "colored people" lived on land that had been granted to them after the Civil War or on land they had inherited from family members to whom it had been granted.

My father employed several of the men from that community as farm hands for $1.00 a day and findings (salt pork, cornmeal, food supplies). We knew it was daybreak when we heard Charlie whistling as he came over the hill. He walked a mile from his home to our farm in the morning and back home again at night. He ate his meals at our house, but by the cultural norms of the community, he could not eat with our family at the same table. He waited until we finished eating. My father would sternly remind us that Charlie was hungry after working all day. Charlie sat and waited on the wood box by the kitchen stove, often yawning. He hardly ever said a word until he left for the night. In a half-melancholy, half-spirited tone he would announce, "Got to get out of here," as he stretched his tired, lank frame.

I also remember Annie, who worked for us and sometimes helped do our washing. My mother gave her as much food as she could carry knowing that her husband was out of work. An indelible memory is of Annie climbing up the hill from our house at the end of the day, carrying a sack of food to her family of small children. She looked as if her back would break.

My parents viewed as reprehensible the suspected lynchings in our county and tried to protect us from hearing about it, but I heard the stories at school. When I rode to school on the bus, I couldn't understand why the "colored" children, as they were called then, had to walk the same route. Before I left Fauquier County in my twenties, I appeared before the school board with a petition for a school bus to transport the African American children to school. By then I had heard the call to social work.

◉ ◉ ◉ ◉ ◉

The Great Depression in the 30s had its unmistakable effects in our Orlean community. Some people who lived through that experience feel they were deprived. Many people

I knew never felt deprived. I am one of the latter. I knew hungry and shivering children at school, and was often reminded by my parents that people were hungry, but I never was.

Although I didn't have a new coat until I went to high school, I had galoshes. Many children I knew wore floppy-soled, wet shoes. An aunt often sent us boxes of old clothes from the city. My mother made my blue serge, pleated skirts and tweed jumpers from men's wool suits. My father tried to help my mother cut out pants for my brother from second-hand clothing, but they gave up the endeavor. My brother proudly wore Sears Roebuck bib overalls, like his dad.

Agriculture was in a crisis all through those days. Farmers were not able to meet the cost of production and have enough money left to pay their debts. The farmer's share of the national income dropped precipitously from fifteen to nine percent between 1920 and 1928. My father's last optimistic fling was to buy a grass green Ford touring car for $500 just before the stock market crash in 1929. I went with him to buy it at the Marshall Motor Company. When we got home, I picked up on his pride and painted his name and address on the side of the new green car with clear varnish. I got a whipping for saying that my brother had done it. I had completed the first grade by then and knew how to write, and my two-year-old brother didn't know the alphabet.

When the first banks began to fail in 1930, and people withdrew their funds from them, my parents almost lost the farm. They couldn't pay the taxes because a cattle dealer went bankrupt and couldn't honor his contract to buy my father's cattle. My mother took in boarders and started raising turkeys. We milked extra cows and sold cream. My father worked even harder. By 1932, the annual per capita farm income was $352. Millions of people in the industrialized economy lost their jobs. Unemployed uncles and aunts, and cousins and their wives came to live with us. The men helped my father on the farm in return for their board for themselves and their wives. One uncle told the story that when he arrived at our home for refuge and saw so many other relatives there, he left even though he was unemployed and had no place to live.

Our household living was comfortable and adequate but never easy compared to modern standards. Like most farm families in rural America then, we had no electricity, running water, or telephone until after I had finished college. We cooked and heated the house using wood stoves. We made laundry soap over an open fire and did our laundry by hand until my mother insisted upon buying a Maytag gasoline washing machine with money from the sale of her turkeys. The one real convenience we had was a dairy with concrete boxes filled with cold water pumped by hand from the well. We got our first ice box in 1938. The hundred pound blocks of ice usually melted before the delivery truck returned.

My mother needed help with the extra work that resulted from taking in boarders. I learned to wash clothes on a wash-board, to rinse and blue and hang them outside on a line, and to iron them with irons heated on a wood stove. Learning to take responsibility for the jobs I enjoyed such as scrubbing the dairy, and jobs I detested, such as feeding the turkeys, pre-pared me for making my own decisions later. I was closely identified with my mother in making and keeping our home attractive in my pre-adolescent years. We cleaned an antique corner cupboard that the chickens had nested in and painted the shelves pink and moved it into our dining room. We made curtains and bedspreads and dressing table skirts. The *piece de resistance* was painting the old linoleum covered floors and sponging them with different colored paints. For a long time, during my adolescent years when I found it embarrassing, we lived in a kitchen painted pumpkin orange and grass green, which my family remembers as the Depression kitchen.

Creative expression, along with a sense of agency and mas-tery, was evidently important for me in those years. Clearing a trail through the pine woods to a huge rock outcropping, and damming a creek are some of my favorite memories. On rare occasions, when friends and cousins came to visit, we put on tent shows with singing and dancing.

When I was eleven, my mother refused to give me piano lessons any longer after I had a temper tantrum at the piano bench because she wouldn't let me improvise. After six years of piano lessons, I continued to practice piano, turning to her occasionally when something puzzled me. While I did not master music, I learned to take pleasure in entertaining myself.

My young life was lived amidst farm accidents, sudden deaths and mental illness. Accidental injuries and deaths were highly visible in a rural community and were traumatic episodes for me. Funerals for individuals who died suddenly, as a result of violence, always made me feel nauseated. They reminded me of my grandmother's funeral, which I attended when I was four.

My preparation for crisis therapy and work with the mentally ill, then viewed as "eccentric" or "crazy," began in those Depression years. I remember sitting up all night with my parents while they tried to help control the violent behavior of a neighbor until the sheriff could transport him to the hospital. That image often surfaced when I later worked in a psychiatric hospital.

Parents of two of my close friends committed suicide in the 30s and 40s. The tragedy of these losses for my friends and their families and for the community lives with me still.

My friends' losses were particularly poignant for me because my father experienced a severe depression and threatened suicide in the late 1930s when I was in high school. My mother looked to me for help in saving his life, a responsibility I was not prepared for. My mother viewed my father's depression as related to his mood swings between despair and exaggerated optimism, but she did not acknowledge or understand his serious emotional condition. I often wondered about my father's struggle to pay for the farm as a factor in his depression.

Medical care in those Depression years was even less accessible than it is today. I remember a medical crisis when I was eleven. Our family doctor made a house call and took my family to the University of Virginia Hospital in Charlottesville, seventy miles away, for clinic care. My mother nearly bled to death with a miscarriage on the way. I had appendicitis. A horse had kicked my father. And my little brother was badly bitten by a dog when my father tried to leave him at a neighbor's house while we went to the hospital. My mother and I were hospitalized in different parts of the hospital. My father had to return home to look after my brother and the farm.

I was absolutely captivated by the medical setting and personnel on a ward of twenty patients—and totally trusting. My parents were told a week later that my appendix had almost ruptured and that an ovarian tumor had been removed. I guess it's not surprising that twenty years later, I began a lengthy stint lasting for twenty-three years working in a hospital setting.

Chapter 3:

FAMILY BACKGROUND, FAMILY HERITAGE

My ancestors, on both sides of my family, lived in or at the base of the Blue Ridge Mountains in Virginia, since before the American Revolution. My parents and extended families were Blue Ridge Mountain storytellers. Stories of helping others came down through the generations and wore away at me like water dripping on stone.

The living conditions and culture of the Blue Ridge Mountain people from pioneer days required that they help one another as a matter of survival. As they said in my family, "It came naturally." A strong sense of interdependency and community developed. Just as problem traits sometimes evolve in families (undoubtedly did in my own), I think it is likely that a predisposition for service to others also evolved. By family heritage and precept, I was prepared for a life of service to others.

My father, Rubert Otto Updike, and my mother, Arthelia Catherine Cullers, were brought up at the turn of the twentieth century in Bentonville, a small village, between the towns

of Front Royal and Luray, in the Shenandoah Valley of
Virginia. The Valley is bounded by the Massanutten mountain
range on one side and the Blue Ridge on the other. The north
fork of the Shenandoah River, then pure and clean, mean-
dered down the valley through seven bends. Known as the
"breadbasket" during the Civil War, the Shenandoah Valley
was a verdant and productive farmland.

My father's family proudly traced their heritage to the
Dutch, who settled New Amsterdam in New York in the
1600s. The Virginia Updikes were descended from John
Opdyke, who settled in Loudon County in 1747. My Updike
ancestors settled in Rappahannock and Warren Counties on
either side of the Blue Ridge Mountains. They frequently
intermarried but also mixed with the Scotch-Irish, who were
early settlers in the Appalachians. Names like Murphy and
Brown appear in the line. The extended family was so large
there was little need for outside contact. Wherever the
Updikes went they could expect a meal or lodging upon their
arrival—"Come on in, cousin. Make yourself at home." They
danced, sang, and talked. They were entertaining storytellers.

My father's parents, Samuel Booten Updike (born 1856)
and Cora Penelope Updike (born 1859), who were distant
cousins, reared their family of seven on a farm near
Bentonville. They were hard working, frugal, and creative people who tilled the soil and made the most of their resources.
Their character exemplified the Quaker traditions of simplicity of lifestyle and generosity of spirit. They staunchly defended the pacifist view of the Quakers.

The Opdyke Genealogy published by Charles Wilson
Opdyke in 1889 (later updated as *The Virginia Updikes-
Updykes*, published by Robert Craig in 1985), was as well
worn as the family Bible. "Optimum Vix Satis" (Truth is Best)
is the Updike family motto. I often wished I didn't have to
hear the unvarnished truth about the plain-speaking, unpre-
tentious Updikes, when I was a child.

My maternal grandfather, Robert Burley Cullers, M.D.,

(born 1863) was the only physician between Front Royal and
Luray. Prior to attending medical school, he had taught a one-
room school in the Blue Ridge Mountains to earn money for
his medical school education in Baltimore. Upon his return,
he married my grandmother, Emma Miller, (born 1869) a
Scotch-Irish lass, whom he had met when he was a teacher.
They settled in Bentonville where he practiced medicine as a
horse and buggy doctor.

Doctor Cullers was a legendary figure in the Shenandoah
Valley. Tales were told of his frosted fingers and his bearskin
gloves. He rode horseback from one house to another during
epidemics of typhoid, diphtheria and influenza. Many babies
that he delivered were named after him. Dr.Cullers' pink pills
were believed to cure many ailments, including neurasthenia.
He deplored the sanitation practices in his village and served
as a self-appointed Public Health Officer to teach methods of
good sanitation. Once he lined up his six children in public
and inoculated them with vaccine to prevent typhoid and to
prove to people in the village that inoculations would not kill
them.

Grandfather Cullers often bartered his medical services with
the mountain people in exchange for honey, chestnuts, huckle-
berries, cherries or other food products. He evidently was not a
good bookkeeper. Many debts owed to him at the time of his
death were never paid. He died at the early age of fifty-seven
leaving my grandmother with insufficient funds to raise and
educate their six children. Nevertheless, my mother and my
aunts and uncles became teachers, ministers and politicians carrying on grandfather's legacy in the helping professions.

My mother, Arthelia Cullers, occupied a special position
in Bentonville. She was Dr. Cullers' daughter. She was dressed
like a lady and went by train with her trunk to finishing school
at Elizabeth College in Salem, Virginia and to Brandon
Institute in Bayse, Virginia. She excelled as an accomplished
pianist and piano teacher. Later, she received a teacher's professional certificate from the teachers college now known as

James Madison University in Harrisonburg, Virginia. She returned to Bentonville to teach and became the principal of Bentonville School from 1919 to 1922 when she left Bentonville after marrying my father.

Known as "Thelia," she was a striking looking young woman with blue eyes and long black hair. She enjoyed riding horseback and playing tennis and preferred reading and playing the piano to housework. She voted the first time women could and took pride in her political independence. In the view of many that knew her, she was one of the early feminists.

My father was an outgoing, energetic, and resourceful young man. He was talented musically and taught himself to play the violin. He loved to sing and dance and liked to pretend he was a vaudeville entertainer. He commanded a repertoire of fiddle tunes, folk songs, World War I songs, Broadway hits, and operatic arias.

My father had kept his eye on Dr. Cullers' daughter through her girlhood and her engagement to a man who was killed in World War I in France. While waiting to pursue her, he served in the Army during that war, and worked in the rubber mills in Akron, Ohio. He returned to Bentonville as a handsome, dynamic, and ambitious fellow in his new Dodge touring car, wearing a diamond stickpin in his tie.

That diamond became my mother's engagement ring in a platinum solitaire setting, which I still cherish today. Music was the medium for my parents' courtship. He had the talent; she had the training. Rubert and Thelia were a popular young couple who entertained friends and families and often played the music for square dances.

They took the morning train from Bentonville to Washington, D.C. to get married on December 20, 1921. My mother wore a midnight blue, serge wool suit and a beaded bronze-colored taffeta hat and blouse, a somber outfit for a bride. Once, on a rainy afternoon, she opened her trunk and showed me the outfit. She told me at that time, about the death of her fiance in France, and that, at my father's suggestion, I was named after him.

My parents brought many of the traditions and values of the Blue Ridge Mountain people with them to Fauquier County. Yet, they made their own distinctive efforts toward individuation. They prided themselves in their newly achieved separate and independent status. I recall many of their conversations in which they spelled out how different they saw themselves, individually and as a family unit, from their families and the way they were brought up.

When they first came to Fauquier County, they played music for square dances, but they were also familiar with the culture of the 20s. I remember a friend of theirs who bobbed her hair and wore short skirts. She taught me how to dance the Charleston. Songs by Gershwin and Hammerstein became as much a part of their repertoire as "Over There" and other World War I songs.

Music filled our summer evenings while we sat in the front porch swings and sang. In the winter, my mother played the piano and my dad played the fiddle by the fire in the parlor. My dad and I wore a spot of varnish off the floor clog dancing. They were always asked to play when company came. The jig, the waltz, ragtime, blues, and eventually, swing became familiar rhythms.

My parents encouraged me to study music, but I never dared to compete with either of them. Still I valued their gift of music. The joy and the rhythm of music are close to the psyche.

My parents took it for granted that helping others was their responsibility. They didn't always enjoy it, and often questioned their own judgment about whether what they offered to others was helpful. My father would complain about having to milk the cows and process the milk for children whose parents refused to take a cow on loan and milk her, but they furnished the milk for the sake of the children. They were often called upon by people who were in crisis or needed transportation for medical care. My mother was empathic and heard people out. My father was more straightforward in his approach, "Here, let me give you a hand."

After my mother stopped teaching at the one room school near our home, she taught Works Progress Administration (WPA) courses for adults during the Depression. She went out into the community to find the students and organized the classes. She was one of my early models in community organization. She continued tutoring persons who were functionally illiterate for the rest of her life. She was a leader in her church and community.

She taught piano lessons and helped some of her students with their college educations. After desegregation in Virginia, she was severely criticized for planning to include African American students in her piano recital at her church. She found a more attractive and receptive site in the community for the recital.

My father was a social person, a good conversationalist, who enjoyed others. He was totally attentive to the other person— child, laborer, stranger, friend. I think of him as a man who struck a fair bargain, and after that, deliberately gave the "other fellow a little more than his fair share."

The Judeo-Christian values and democratic principles my parents lived by were deeply instilled in me in my early years. Their responsibility for citizenship, their compassion for others, their generosity and hospitality, their faith in God, and their optimism about the human condition became a part of me. Their endurance, resiliency, physical stamina, sense of humor, and capacity to enjoy what life granted them, was truly remarkable.

Chapter 4:

WHEATLEY SCHOOL TO MARY WASHINGTON COLLEGE

Wheatley School was a seven-grade, one-room school located a half-mile from our home. My mother was the teacher there from 1922 until 1930, when the school was closed. Big boys in their teens, little tykes with their tin lunch pails, trudged miles, through all kinds of weather, to get to school. After it closed, the children were transported by a school bus to either Orlean or Hume schools.

My first two years of school at Wheatley set the tone for my performance as "the teacher's pet" during the rest of my public school days. My mother did not want to take me to school with her when I was five years old, a year before I was school age, and I did not want to go. But Rainey, our new housekeeper that year, claimed she was hired to take care of my baby brother exclusively, and refused to take care of me because she thought I was a spoiled child. Rainey threatened to "put spiders in my bread."

Some of my memories of Wheatley are vivid. My first playmates and friends, Virginia and Helen, and I made mud pies, and we lined up as teams with the big children to shout political slogans, "Hoover, Hoover sitting on the fence, waiting for Smith to give him some sense." I hold the image of a spelling bee and the hushed sounds in the schoolroom as I triumphantly outspelled a seventh grader with the word "sincerely."

A vaguer memory is of the shame I felt at being punished by my mother, the teacher, for behavior that was provoked and reported by the older children. My mother took a small branch from a tree and switched me in the presence of all the children. Later, she kept me in at recess, took me on her lap to comfort me in my distraught state and explained she could not treat me preferentially. She had already had the experience of teaching her younger siblings in Bentonville.

For grammar school and three years of high school I attended Hume School. Most of the time, I found a way, usually by conformity, pleasing manners and superior performance, to be known as the teacher's pet. The teacher's approval was exceedingly important to me. My brother claims today that his teachers always expected his maximum performance, like that of his sister before him.

Hume school was a five-room, red brick country schoolhouse. It was ten miles from our home. The school bus had to make two trips over dirt roads. Walking a mile, each way, to and from the bus, through the woods, called for mastery of my personal resources. I insisted on going to school regardless of the weather. Once I suffered frostbitten fingers and toes while waiting for the school bus that never came, because the bus driver couldn't start the engine in zero degree weather.

Hume High School laid a base for my liberal arts education for which I have always been grateful. Benjamin Burgess Mitchell, an exceptional teacher, was there only because he had no other work during the Depression. He would stop us in world history class to ask the question with his intense dark eyes flashing, "*What* is life? What *is* life? What is *life*?" From him I learned the word "proantidisestablishmentarianism."

My graduation from the third year of high school in June 1939, was the marker between the awkwardness of adolescence and the pain of youth. I remember standing at the lectern, delivering my valedictory address for my class of seven. My voice rang out clear and strong. I was wearing a white, silk shantung dress that I had designed myself. I was embarrassed that the dress did not fit properly, that it was too loose in the waist.

At fifteen, I had a crush on my high school teacher, Meriwether Blair Dickinson, and assumed I was his favorite. He was a handsome young man, just out of college, a romantic at heart, who read the poetry of Keats and Shelly to us and challenged us to love great literature.

I was bereft at telling Mr. Dickinson good-bye. I thought I could not bear never seeing him again, for it was known that he was planning to join the Navy. For a week, my despair was inconsolable. I moped and I wept. My mother tried to distract my attention to the dotted swiss dress she was making for me to wear to attend a senior prom at Marshall High School with my real boy friend, Dick. Dick had followed the school bus in his cream truck, hoping to see me, at the same time I had followed Mr. Dickinson in my fantasy.

My senior year of high school in Marshall was emotionally stormy. It was not easy for me to adjust to a class of twenty-nine students. I could not take part in extra-curricular activities because I rode the school bus. I felt self-conscious among my classmates, but I managed to take a lead role in the senior play and was runner-up for first place in the beauty contest.

◉   ◉   ◉   ◉   ◉

My parents and teachers had always assumed I would go to college. In high school, the question became "which college?" I was disappointed that my parents could not afford to send me to a private school, but I soon began to think of Mary

Washington College in Fredricksberg, fifty miles from home.

After my application was accepted, my father took me to the Marshall National Bank to apply for a personal loan. Trips to the bank with my father, for loans during the Depression, made that a familiar setting. Press Anderson, the bank president, and my father, solemnly explained the seriousness of taking a loan and projected into the future the many years it might take me to pay off this loan. It took me ten years.

Mary Washington College was the women's college of the University of Virginia when I went there from 1940 to 1944. It was a state-supported liberal arts school with a total enrollment of about 2000. Named after the mother of George Washington, it was located on a hill overlooking the historic sites in the town of Fredericksburg. It had a beautiful campus with brick buildings of colonial architecture, lush woodland of trees and greenery and iron gates, which closed at ten o'clock at night.

The campus provided a protected setting for making friends, some of whom have remained close to me throughout my life.

My college years smoothed some of the rough edges of my adolescence and helped me mature. Socializing had a higher priority for me than studying. My favorite recollection of Mary Washington is multiplied by the many "Hellos." Each of us always spoke to students or faculty members approaching from the opposite direction. No matter what the mood or the weather, a friendly greeting was in order. It was not surprising how many of the other students we got to recognize by name.

I had different roommates each year. My sophomore year in 1941-1942 was the most memorable. Five of us shared a two-bedroom suite with a tiny closet kitchen in Betty Lewis Hall, one of the oldest dormitories on campus. Our personalities and backgrounds were a study in diversity. Ruth was chosen as a member of the May Queen's Court because of her outstanding beauty, leadership, and popularity. Maresy was bright, intellectual, a straight A student who looked and acted more mature than the rest of us. Co was bright, cute, with her big, round blue eyes, her extensive collection of sweaters, which furnished a perfect back drop for fraternity pins. June was more interested in her weekend trips off campus to Cornell University to meet Bob, to whom she was pinned, than she was in our campus life. And I was a southern, country girl who was less sophisticated than any of them. All of the others were from the north—New Jersey, New York City, Connecticut and New York State. They took me on as a project, to overhaul my southern accent and diction, and taught me how to study.

On December 7, 1941, when the Japanese bombed Pearl Harbor, all five of us became adults. My suitemates and I were permanently bonded in our collective recollection of that event.

I sometimes think of Mary Washington as like the finishing schools my mother attended in the South in the early part of this century. We ate by candlelight and frequently had instrumental or vocal music as entertainment. Teas, tea dances, and formal dances were a big part of campus life.

Our dean of women, Mrs. Bushnell, expected us to act like "young ladies" and taught us how to hold our soup spoons and how to dip our soup. All young men who visited the campus needed the written recommendation of the parents of the student they were visiting. When we had a date, he was received by Mrs. B before he proceeded to greet us in our dormitory parlor.

My socialization and learning to be a young lady extended beyond the Mary Washington campus. Friends invited me to visit their homes for weekends in Richmond and New York. College men and servicemen visited our campus. Some of my most memorable visits to other campuses included trips on the train to Virginia Polytechnic Institute for football games and big band dances, football games and dances at the University of Virginia, and June Week at the U.S. Naval Academy in Annapolis.

At the time, I thought of my education at Mary Washington as preparation for marriage. But as the years went by and I understood that the real goal of a liberal arts college is the broader one of preparation for life, I have often been reminded of some of the unforgettable learning experiences that opened up a thirst for knowledge that has yet to be satisfied: helping Hugo Iltis, Ph.D., my biology professor, set up his Mendelian Museum (he had brought his precious artifacts of Gregory Mendel's experiments with peas out of Czechoslovakia just before World War II began); Dr. Gordon Moss's rumbling bass voice as he brought us into the drama of American history; a firm grasp of the scientific method in laboratory experiments; hearing a symphony for the first time.

When social work became my chosen profession, I found the foundation I had acquired in the humanities to be much more solid than I had imagined. That base provided a firm footing on which to build my personal life and an extra dimension in understanding others.

My class graduated in June 1944, just before D-Day when the allied forces invaded Normandy. My classmates and I have often speculated about why our experience at Mary Washington College had such a special meaning. I think it has to do with our experience of wartime. Together, we experienced the news of Pearl Harbor and of the Declaration of War. We learned what blackouts were like. We regularly donated blood to the Blood Bank, entertained hundreds of men in uniform on our campus, and said goodbye to some of them forever.

Merle at age 20, upon graduation from Mary Washington
College in 1944

Fauquier County Courthouse
Warrenton, Virginia

II. THE CALL

Fauquier County Welfare Department

1944-1946

Chapter 5:

CHOICE OR CHANCE

When I graduated from college I found that there were unprecedented employment opportunities for women during that crucial period of World War II. Once more back on the farm, I yearned to work in the defense industry or join the WAVES (Women Accepted for Volunteer Emergency Service, U.S. Navy) or the Red Cross, but my first social work mentor appeared at my front door. Lina Cameron came to complete my mother's foster home study and charmed me into applying for an entry level social work job at the Fauquier County Welfare Department. I wasn't going to be easy pickings. Lina's efforts to recruit me were at odds with my more exotic ideas.

My classmates were joining the armed services. Defense industries were recruiting chemists. My friend Ruth was going to Texas to work in a military hospital as a dietetic intern. Another friend, Ginia, was learning to be a medical technician. I was considering employment as a chemist for which I had filed applications with DuPont Ltd., and the U.S. Bureau of Standards. Joining the war effort attracted me. I could hardly wait to make a trip to Washington, D.C. to explore joining the WAVES and other options.

While I was finishing college, Lina Cameron was brought to Fauquier County as an outside expert to close down the Children's Home, the poorhouse for children. Funds had become available for foster care and Aid to Dependent Children as a result of the Social Security Act of 1935. She was recruiting social workers and seeking applicants to become foster home parents.

Lina Cameron had earned her credentials as a WPA social worker and as a disaster worker for the American Red Cross. She was an attractive, middle-aged woman whose Southern charm and friendly manner quickly captivated the town's leaders. Her candor and sense of humor conveyed warmth as a part of her professional demeanor with clients, staff and board members. She was also a savvy politician. It seemed to me that with her steely blue eyes she could see straight through the questionable motivation of a politician, or a client, or even the town's widower who tried to put the make on her. She was as skilled at negotiating agency budgets with the County Board of Supervisors as she was at obtaining the necessary financial support for a client from the Welfare Board. She read widely and sought out whatever professional training she could find.

She had already recruited Arabelle Laws Arrington, my "big sister" at Mary Washington, for one of the social worker positions. Upon learning I had arrived home, as a new college graduate with some psychology and sociology background, she, and Arabelle, set their sights upon me as a "native daughter" for the other vacant social worker position. Soon Lina's networking skills, as they might be called today, drew others in to recruit me.

When I arrived at the Welfare Department for the job application interview, my qualifications had been thoroughly researched and, it appeared I was viewed as the ideal candidate. Arabelle recommended me without qualification. Sam

Hall, the county sheriff and a family friend, Press Anderson, president of the Marshall National Bank, and Will McCarty, the chairman of the local welfare board, and a farmer like my father, all vouched for my character and what they viewed as my politically conservative upbringing.

The welfare board, at a meeting, which was scheduled for the same day as my application interview, was prepared to hire me. John G. Howell, the district representative from the State Department of Public Welfare, and Flora Yowell, a child welfare representative from Richmond, were present to interview me and to encourage me to take the job.

Lina Cameron held out a strong hand of support. She told me she viewed me as "bright, sensitive, and someone with heart." But she also recognized my lack of experience and immaturity and forewarned me that I might be viewed as a "soft touch for political manipulation." In my naiveté, I was not sure what that meant.

I was impressed by their overwhelming vote of confidence. I thanked them with the girlish sincerity of the ingenue that I was and politely turned down the job in order to explore other options. Flora Yowell, an attractive, fashionably dressed, and articulate woman, later that day, wisely offered to drive me to Washington, D.C. for my upcoming interviews there. As we drove along in her smart looking roadster, Flora described the child welfare field and the need for young persons, such as myself, to take on the challenge. It was enticing; I was dimly aware that her professional demeanor was attracting my ego ideal of a person with a professional identity.

In Washington, I turned down the WAVES recruitment officer's offer upon learning, to my surprise, that there was no guarantee that I would be trained as a laboratory technician or that I would be stationed in the Washington area. I politely agreed to consider the chemist position offered by the Bureau of Standards but at the conclusion of my application interview, I was stunned at the grim scene I had encountered. The chemist, who interviewed me, a haggard looking man informed me that he hadn't slept for forty-eight hours. He told me that the person who previously occupied the position I was being considered for had been injured in an experiment. The damage to the building was still visible in the form of a broken wall and the disarray of the laboratory. On the same trip, I filed applications for high school teaching jobs in Fairfax and Stafford Counties, and for a brain wave technician job at the University of Virginia Hospital.

Then, three days later, as I was returning home, I reached a decision, made as some of the most important decisions of our lives are made, from a deeply intuitive level. I remember the instant vividly as I rode home on the Trailway bus through my native Virginia countryside, so beautifully green in summer. I could name the spot in the road. I knew from the bottom of my heart I wanted to work with people—not laboratory test tubes and beakers. I had heard the call to social work.

Chapter 6:

THE AWAKENING

I can still see myself on the way to work in my first job as a social worker, on a bright summer morning in June, 1944. Driving along Lee Highway, south to Warrenton, in my pre-war 1939 Oldsmobile coupe, I was stunned by the brilliance of the dew laden blue cornflowers on either side of the road and blinked back the tears. A news commentator on the car radio was describing the casualties and bloodshed on the Normandy Beach from D-Day.

Already, my childhood sweetheart, Harfield Brown, had been killed at Anzio Beach in Italy, and a friend's fiance who was a pilot, had been shot down in the Pacific. My sense of loss was covered over by my excitement at being alive and my anticipation of my new adventure. At the age of twenty-one, I was reaching toward the idealistic challenge of healing wounds I knew existed in the war-torn world, and wounds I knew, at some level, existed in my own community and in my own internal psyche.

The label of do-gooder, that is often attached to the social

worker who leaves old clothes for the poor at the country
store, had no more appeal for me then than it does now. I
wanted to find a way to work with people as my intuitive flash
had informed me was my calling. My curiosity and observa-
tional acuity had been whetted in sociology classes at Mary
Washington, but my questions about motivation, about what
"made people tick," were still not answered.

The three-room Welfare Department office, where I was
to work, was located on the ground floor in the historic
Fauquier County Courthouse next to the jail, the Fauquier
County National Bank, and the historic Warren Green Hotel.
The Courthouse Square was an exciting place to work.
Attorneys, secretaries, dentists, and shopkeepers greeted one
another with a cheerful "Good morning," to start the day.

My day began with my supervisory conference with Lina
Cameron, my first casework supervisor and mentor. She provided a humorous and philosophical introductory short
course in the basic principles and values of social work. She
raised ethical issues I needed to consider and prepared me for
standing up for the rights of my clients. She alerted me to
some of the shockers that might offend my tender sensibilities
when I made home visits and helped me anticipate attitudes I
could expect to encounter interviewing references.

Lina was a woman whose sensitivity and experience in living allowed her to be both tough and tender. Her self-awareness and her acceptance of others with their strengths and limitations inspired me. Her skill at creating a climate of growth
and change made me feel I was a responsible person.

Lina assigned my caseload of more than a hundred cases in
stacks of ten to fifteen case records at a time. These cases included Aid to Dependent Children (ADC), Old Age Assistance
(OAA), Aid to The Blind (AB), Aid to The Disabled (ATD), cat-
egories established by the Social Security Act, and General Relief,
which was funded with County funds. It was my responsibility
as a caseworker to help clients establish their eligibility for public assistance or help them understand why they were not eligi-

ble. I also obtained the social histories of men who were drafted for the armed services, for the Selective Service Board. That was my first experience in gathering information for case histories.

My job required me to do a lot of traveling to make home visits to persons applying for or receiving public assistance, and collateral visits to references and family members. Much of my travel was over dirt roads, which were often dusty or, during the rainy season, flooded. Once I was caught in a rainstorm and marooned on the top of Cobbler Mountain until a search party found me.

My assigned territory was the Upper End of Fauquier County, which included Marshall, The Plains, Rectortown, Upperville, Markham, Linden, Hume, and a few other small villages. This was the part of the county I knew best. I had studied its geography in school, and on the school bus to Hume and Marshall, but much of it I had not seen. I began to view Fauquier County through a new lens that highlighted the beauty of the countryside and uncovered appalling social conditions. The magnificent homes and estates in the horse country were a striking contrast to the dilapidated houses in the back woods and mountains. I saw pockets of extreme poverty at the edge of some of the villages. Within ten miles of where I was brought up, I visited homes in which the ground was used as floors and the windows were stuffed with newspapers. Ragged children cried out in hunger. Even more disturbing were the expressions of apathy, helplessness, and hopelessness that I saw on many faces.

The class distinctions and racial prejudice, with which I had grown up, took on new meaning. Employers, references, and benefactors of my clients often had attitudes that placed people on a value scale measuring them by what they "deserved." The English Poor Laws were not passe in Fauquier County.

The lessons I learned from my work in Fauquier County, under the tutelage of Lina Cameron, are recalled here as vignettes, representing patterns of human experience that have endured. They also illustrate principles of social work.

Person In Social Situation

Nanni, a young mother who received Aid to Dependent Children, was bereaved by the accidental death of her tenant farmer husband. Her aged parents lived in her home. Her bedridden father was on Old Age Assistance and her blind mother received Aid to the Blind. She was distraught and overwhelmed. "A poor manager," her landlord, the owner of the farm said. He pressured the Welfare Department Board to move her out of his tenant house. I talked with him and persuaded the chairman of the Welfare Board to talk with him. Our efforts at intervention failed.

I found the condition of Nanni's home shocking—seven people living in two small rooms, sick children, sickening smells, and filth. Despite Lina's warning that there was little I could do to change the complexity of the circumstances, I wanted to save Nanni. I set out with mop and bucket, on my own time, on Saturday, to help her clean her house, hoping that a more orderly household would help persuade the landlord to let her family remain throughout the winter. My efforts didn't work and the eviction proceeded as scheduled.

Little did I know of crisis intervention, or grief therapy, or how humiliated and offended Nanni would be by my poorly conceived efforts of support. Several years later, when I was working for the State Department of Public Welfare in Richmond, I learned that Nanni's children had arrived at the Children's Bureau for care as dependent and neglected children. Their mother had been committed to the state mental hospital.

I never forgot the lesson that some persons are caught in situations over which they have no control. Nor did I forget that I had not known how to engage Nanni in a collaborative effort to preserve her dignity and her sanity and save her family.

The Dignity and Worth of Every Human Being

Marta, a sturdy looking middle-aged woman and her two blind sons, came to town once a month to pick up the Aid to The Blind checks for her sons. Sometimes, neighbors brought them; sometimes, they walked seven miles from their isolated, backwoods village—Marta in her work clothes and heavy boots and the blind sons with their walking sticks. Marta was known for her straightforward manner. She championed her sons' right to Public Assistance and demonstrated her appreciation for their benefits and medical care. Marta had lost several children in their early years because medical care was not available. I remembered one of them who died of mastoiditis; he was a classmate of mine when I was in grammar school.

Marta was a hard working woman who earned a dollar a day as a field hand in crop season, planting or cutting corn, and was recognized by her work boots and the gunny sacks she swung on her back.

I learned many lessons from Marta, but perhaps the most basic was learning to appreciate her dignity and strength as a human being. She was under attack in the farm community for "not being worthy" of the Public Assistance for which her blind sons were eligible. I defended her at Welfare Board meetings, at my church, and among neighbors and friends. In doing so, I learned both advocacy and the basic principle she so magnificently demonstrated—the dignity and worth of every individual.

Self and Other—the Casework Relationship

One of my responsibilities was to certify eligibility for medical care for General Relief clients and to arrange transportation for them by the Red Cross. One bright autumn day, as I hiked up the mountain back of Linden through moonshine territory, I came upon a still. A man with a shotgun chased me off the premises because he was wary of "revenuers" or strangers, in general. At that moment, my client appeared and assured me I had nothing to fear. Dressed in rags, he stretched out his hands toward me in a gesture of welcome and entreaty. There was a hole in his face where his nose had once been. His body was seeping fluids that were no longer under his control.

Later, I learned my client was suffering with tertiary syphilis. "There but for the grace of God go I," was Lina Cameron's consolation. She helped me to see that my willingness to complete my interpersonal transaction with him had probably offered him some measure of comfort and support, that there was mutuality in our exchange.

The profound effect of World War II sometimes made it seem that the suffering I saw in my home county was a microcosm of the world picture. While we were told little of the larger suffering in the world, during the war because of wartime secrecy, I had welcomed home a friend whose body still carried shrapnel from D-Day, and a neighbor who was sent home from the Pacific with malaria in the summer of 1944. Friends were dying in Europe and in the Pacific. Sending my brother off to the Navy when he enlisted on his eighteenth birthday struck close to my heart.

But I have many good memories of working in Warrenton and Fauquier County and of the warm friendliness of the people I got to know.

I soon felt a part of the activity in the courthouse square and began making friends. One of my more memorable experiences was attending a dinner party at the National Press Club in Washington, D.C. Sir Alexander Fleming, who discovered penicillin, was the speaker. This trip with friends was a thrilling experience for me because I was such a social novice. I found Fleming's discovery exciting as I thought about the implications of the use of penicillin in wartime.

Most of Fauquier County's young men were away in the service. The young women who worked in Warrenton invited me to join them as hostesses at well-chaperoned, formal dances for servicemen at the U.S.O. and at the historic Warren Green

Hotel. We developed a real sense of camaraderie.

The soldiers we entertained from Vint Hill Army Signal Corps Station were special—bright, attractive and well educated. After the war, it became public knowledge that the men at Vint Hill broke the secret code of the Japanese military forces. Many hearts in Fauquier County were also broken; mine was one of them.

The Vint Hill men found me attractive; perhaps it was because I had an automobile and gasoline, which was strictly rationed. I transported four of them around to sing as a barbershop quartet at civic functions, after which they were entertained at homes of Fauquier County citizens. I dated several of these servicemen.

At Christmastime in 1944, I fell in love with Joe, a soldier from Vint Hill. There was little time to get acquainted before he was transferred to another station. We corresponded in long, romantic letters expressing our feelings about one another, the wartime we lived in, poetry, literature, life. I had not been in such a romantic state since I was sixteen when I thought I was in love with my high school teacher.

Joe hitchhiked back and forth to Warrenton and spent a week with me, at my parents' home, before he went overseas. My mother told me later that she had questioned the advisability of his visits. But she remembered her own experience in World War I, in which she had entertained her fiance in her parents' home before he went overseas, and was later killed in France. After Joe's last visit, he sent me a beautifully bound book of poetry, *A Shropshire Lad* by A.E. Housman and marked the lines:

> "When I was one and twenty
> I heard a wise man say
> Give crowns and pounds and guineas
> But not your heart away
> Give pearls away and rubies
> But keep your fancy-free."

That was a prophetic admonition. For many years, no matter how much I tried to tell myself I cared about someone else, Joe was always on my mind.

The intense personal memories of my twenty-first and twenty-second years, back home in Fauquier County, converged with the celebration of the end of World War II and peace. My friends and I celebrated V.J. day at the Warrenton House at Fauquier Springs with a champagne dinner. The Four Freedoms articulated by Franklin D. Roosevelt—Freedom of Expression, Freedom of Religion, Freedom from Want and Freedom from Fear—and incorporated in the United Nation's Charter, were profoundly meaningful to me as I thought of the people I had known as my clients in Fauquier County. I became more aware of internal pulls and what was going on inside myself. I was more in touch with my feelings, my heartstrings. I felt more alive, sentient, responsible.

Marriage or Career? —Merle examining the engagement ring of her friend and classmate Katherine Lee, 1950

Merle at age twenty-five in
Arlington, Virginia, 1948

Attending a child Welfare League Conference 1952—
Mentors, John G. Howell, 4th from left top row;
Lina Cameron, last on right bottom row

III. INITIATION

Life in Work, Work in Life

1946-1956

Chapter 7:

CHILD WELFARE

Children's Bureau, Richmond, Virginia 1946-1948
Arlington County Welfare Department
Arlington, Virginia 1948-1956

> *You are a wheel at which I stand,*
> *whose dark spokes sometimes catch me up,*
> *revolve me nearer to the center.*
> *Then all the work I put my hand to*
> *widens from turn to turn*
>
> —Rainer Maria Rilke
> (Translated by Anita Barrows and Johanna Macy)

I left home in my twenties to take child welfare jobs first in Richmond, and two years later in Arlington, in the metropolitan Washington, D.C. area. It was my first experience living in an urban environment, an exciting challenge. Child Welfare captured my interest with a vise-like grip and led me into master's graduate training on a Child Welfare Fellowship.

Enormous effort and enthusiasm drew people into the field of social work during that postwar period, when public agencies, schools of social work, and the social work profession joined forces to recruit and train social workers. The Depression and the passage of the Social Security Act had made it clear that more social workers were needed. World War II and the Veterans Administration had demonstrated the need for trained social workers.

Child welfare provided a powerful draw on my youthful idealism, an opportunity to do something about the needs of the children I worked with. My interest grew and deepened as I learned more about human behavior and human development. My work was my joy, my passion, my reason for being. My choice of social work as my profession was one from which I never turned back, a choice I never regretted, but, as I see it now, the personal cost in those early adulthood years was great.

Again, as had been true in the Fauquier County Welfare Department, I was recruited by the Children's Bureau, a big state agency, and by the Arlington County Welfare Department. My first supervisors and teachers were professionally trained social workers, who provided a stimulating atmosphere for learning and lent one hundred percent support to my professional training.

The co-directors of the Children's Bureau were Lois Benedict, a Smith School of Social Work graduate, and Wilhelmina Baughman, a graduate of the University of Pennsylvania School of Social Work. They were as different in personality and temperament as the diagnostic and functional schools of thought from which they came.

In the 1940s, a schism developed in social casework practice. This split was between the ideas and practices of the "Functional School," which were based on the work of Otto Rank, and those of the majority of social work casework practitioners who adhered to the Freudian theory, and called themselves the "Diagnostic Group."

Lois Benedict, who was of the Diagnostic Group, was a

tall, dignified, quiet-mannered woman who wore broad-brimmed picture hats, flowered print dresses, white gloves, and pearls. Willie Baughman, of the Functional School, had a friendly, outgoing manner. She wore well-tailored suits, silk blouses with chunky silver jewelry, and was stylishly classical looking in her appearance.

Although both of them appeared self-confident and strong in their leadership roles, I saw Lois Benedict as the thinker and planner, and Willie Baughman as the more practical hands-on administrator, who negotiated and expedited the solutions to problems. For all their differences, they were models of professional decorum and, together, formed a complementary administration.

In no time, they had me signed up for part-time graduate courses in casework and the history of psychiatry at the Richmond School of Social Work, then a part of the Richmond Professional Institute, College of William and Mary. I can still see Cordelia Cox, a dynamic and inspiring teacher, as she stood before the class wearing an expectant, enthusiastic expression. She encouraged us to speak about social casework principles that were demonstrated in our case material. I first learned about Jung and Freud from a Veteran's Administration psychiatrist who took us to see the Williamsburg State Mental Hospital, one of the first mental hospitals in the United States.

Young college graduates from all over the state of Virginia were arriving at Children's Bureau for training. Soon we were looking at catalogues of schools of social work and thinking about full-time graduate training at some of the better known schools of social work—Smith, New York School of Social Work, the University of Chicago, the University of Pennsylvania.

The Virginia State Department of Public Welfare established the Children's Bureau in Richmond for the protection and care of children who were homeless, dependent and neglected, as well as for those who were in danger of becoming delinquent. These children came from counties that had no provision for their care. Under the Social Security Act, the U.S. Children's Bureau allotted money to states for establishing, supporting, and extending Child Welfare Services, particularly, in rural areas.

The Commonwealth of Virginia put together a program that was the state of the art for the 40s. Administrative and supervisory staff were trained social workers. An interdisciplinary team, including a pediatrician, psychologists, nurses, and social workers evaluated children upon their arrival. A child guidance clinic was available for referral and consultation. But limited financial resources and personnel, large caseloads, and very disturbed children made it a demanding setting to work in.

My job was to supervise foster home placements for individual children and small groups of children in rural counties surrounding Richmond—Chesterfield, Hanover, Henrico, Stafford, Spotsylvania and Louisa Counties. Dirt roads, red clay mud, broom sedge, and borderline poverty characterized the rural communities I visited. Tobacco was the main crop grown. The effect of the Depression was still evident in unpainted houses and dilapidated automobiles and trucks. People grew and canned their vegetables and often supplemented their food supply with wild game—rabbits, birds, deer.

A home study unit of the Children's Bureau had carefully selected these homes for the compassionate and caring attitudes of the foster parents and their capacity for growth in working with disturbed children. The foster parents taught me about empathy. They knew it was painful for children to be so far from home, separated from their families, and respected the children's pain. Take care in removing children from their homes, families, and communities was the lesson etched on my heart.

It seemed to me, I spent more time retrieving adolescent runaway boys from the Juvenile Detention Center in

Richmond and in searching for one more foster home willing to give them a try, than I did working with the boys. Often, they were trying to run away from the foster homes to return to their own homes. Good foster homes for adolescent boys with histories of delinquency were not easy to find or keep. But some of the foster parents succeeded because they had learned not to experience a child's failure to adjust in their home as their own personal failure.

One of the foster homes I remember was Miss Annie Sander's home for six boys between the ages of eight and twelve years. She was a retired schoolteacher who lived in a beautiful old colonial home that she had equipped with bunk beds and separate closets for their possessions. Each boy had the responsibility for his own pet and chores that included making his own bed and a time for help with his homework. One night a week was devoted to writing letters home to their families. Families were encouraged to visit, but few did because they lived so far away.

Some of the boys had serious emotional problems for which they were in treatment at the Child Guidance Clinic in Richmond. Some of them had behavioral problems such as fire setting or stealing, and some had been committed to the Children's Bureau by the juvenile courts as a result of delinquent behavior.

I helped Miss Annie understand the boys' problems and backgrounds. She helped me to see each one of them as a unique child with his own special potential. For a long time I kept a snapshot of six bright-eyed boys, tossing their caps in the air, and wondered how they turned out.

Another foster home I visited was a farm home deep in the red mud territory of Louisa County, at least fifty miles from Richmond. The children placed there were infants and small children with special problems. Among these children was a baby who had pyloric stenosis, a congenital condition that caused projectile vomiting, and a four-year-old boy who had repeatedly run away from home on his tricycle.

It was my responsibility to take the baby to a pediatric

clinic and the little boy to the Child Guidance Clinic for psychotherapy in Richmond. Without the foster mother's help, I
never could have managed it. The baby's distress was inconsolable despite the foster mother's patient effort to soothe him.
It took both of us to manage the hyperactive behavior of the
four-year-old boy. The trip gave us time for getting acquainted and learning together about the children. Many years later,
my recollection of that baby was invaluable in my work as a
psychotherapist, as I tried to understand a patient who had a
history of pyloric stenosis in his infancy.

When I needed to register the baby at the pediatric clinic
before 8:00 A.M., I drove to the little town of Louisa the night
before and stayed in the historic Louisa Courthouse Hotel.
The hotel once had been used as a summer resort for people
to get out of the heat of Richmond. It was still a picture from
the old south with its Georgian architecture, porticos, and tall
ceilings. I remember being awakened by the birds singing outside in the early morning. The breakfasts of steaming hot
cakes, grits, bacon, and fried apples were a sturdy and deli-
cious start for a long day.

For those trips to Louisa, I carefully dressed to fit my
image of a proper, stylish, traveling social worker wearing a hat
and gloves. The first time I had dinner at a cafe across the
street from the hotel, the local swains descended upon the
place and for weeks afterward pursued me when I was back in
Richmond. I saw my popularity as an opportunity for exercis-
ing my discretion in choosing men I wanted to date. They
viewed my motivation quite differently; they apparently saw
me as a woman traveling alone in the Old South.

◉ ◉ ◉ ◉ ◉

My next venture in the Arlington County Department of
Public Welfare established the cornerstone of my professional
career and moved me into graduate training. I worked there as
a child welfare worker before attending graduate school, and,

for a year, between my two years of graduate school. Upon my completion of graduate training in 1953, I became the child welfare supervisor, a position I held until the end of 1956. By that time, I had completed my fellowship obligation, which was to work in child welfare twice as long as I was in graduate school.

In Arlington, as in Richmond, my supervisors, mentors, and teachers were professionally trained social workers. John G. Howell, the director of the Arlington Welfare Department, saw to it that I finished my professional training. He was a graduate of the University of North Carolina School of Social Work, which was then known for its focus on public administration. He took pride in building a model welfare department in urban northern Virginia, and in a professionally trained staff.

John G. Howell's administrative style included careful selection of staff, in-service training, delegation of authority, and fiscal accountability. His top priority was public relations. John G. was known for his hearty sense of humor. With an open door policy for help and support when needed, his laughter could be heard throughout the building. We kidded him about being a frustrated mechanic, because, single-handedly, he kept our fleet of six automobiles running to save public expense.

Marion McCraney, a Smith School of Social Work graduate and a psychiatric social worker, personified the dignity of the profession for me. She was an attractive, sensitive, well-balanced young woman who valued her marriage, as well as her work, and became a personal and professional role model. She supervised me before and between my two years of graduate school. She supervised my first experience in supervising students and modeled how it should be done. She also encouraged me to evaluate my strengths and limitations and helped me to move toward my psychoanalysis.

The Washington, D.C. area offered an extraordinary selection of professionally trained social workers, usually wives of

U.S. government or armed service personnel. My colleagues were trained by some of the best schools of social work in the country at that time—the University of Chicago, Smith, the New York School of Social Work, the University of California School of Social Welfare, and the National Catholic School of Social Service. I treasured my opportunity to learn from these colleagues. A mutually supportive sense of camaraderie made a friendly setting for staff in the welfare department. Some of the most enduring friendships of my life were from that time.

Title V, part 3, of the Social Security Act, entitled Child Welfare Services, which made grants to the states through the U.S. Children's Bureau, strengthened local child welfare services to include foster care, adoptions, and preventive and remedial casework for families and children. All of these programs were included in child welfare services in Arlington. More than half of the welfare department's caseload was made up of child welfare service cases.

The primary focus was on adoptions when I arrived in 1948. In the post World War II era, many families were seeking to adopt children. At the same time, before the birth control pill, many unmarried mothers sought to place their infants in adoption. The Arlington Welfare Department supervised for the court each year, several hundred independent adoptions (adoption placements made outside licensed child placement agencies).

We established what was then an innovative adoption program for a public agency. It included casework services for unmarried mothers, foster home care for their infants, adoptive home studies, placement of children in adoptive homes, and supervision of the placements for the first year before adoptions became final.

We carefully observed the development of infants released for adoption using the help of private pediatricians, psychologists, and foster parents in an effort to get a good match between the children and adoptive parents. We studied dozens of adoptive home applications for every infant released by the natural parent for adoption.

Our adoption program also included participation in a United States Children's Bureau research project that studied the early development of infants placed in adoption. We had mutual agreements with adoption agencies in other states to participate in multi-cultural, multi-racial adoption placements, and placements of physically and emotionally handicapped children, and older children in adoption.

As I look back at those years, visual images of infants and older children I placed in adoption are as clear in my mind as if they were my own children. For a long time, I kept snapshots of some of the infants I placed in foster homes at birth and later placed for adoption in their permanent homes. A friend saw one of those pictures of me holding a baby in my arms and solicitously inquired about whether I had a secret I wanted to share. She thought the child was mine.

Placing a child for adoption was a moving experience as one considered the feelings of the natural mother who had relinquished custody of the infant, the foster mother who had started the infant on its way, and the adoptive parents who welcomed the child with joy. The responsibility for observing the infant's responses in the placement process and for using these observations in the decision making process about a child's life, was humbling for me when I considered it was like playing God.

Modern research on early infant development has borne out the guidelines upon which we based our final decision about whether to place a child with a particular set of parents. Several of us carefully observed the child's particular behavior, which sought a response from the prospective adoptive parents and their response to that behavior.

I think of one example of the complexity of factors that entered into placing a child for adoption. Baby G. was born with a congenital malformation of her hips and legs. She was tentatively relinquished at birth by her natural mother on the condition that this malformation could be corrected. The mother did not want to give final consent until she knew her child was all right.

Baby G., whose family background and early development gave great promise of an exceptional child, unfortunately, was placed in a foster home with three other small children. The foster mother could not give Baby G. the special attention she needed. Baby G. lived in an immobilizing brace to correct her hips and legs for the first five months of her life before a medical release and final relinquishment for adoption could be obtained.

Much preliminary effort had gone into finding adoptive parents, who could meet the special needs of this child, before we arranged for the first set of prospective adoptive parents to see her. Upon finding there was no way they could console her, they refused to consider her. We carefully sought the next set of parents before exposing her to being refused again. This time, she cried as before, but sensing the parents' patience and desire to comfort her, she began to cuddle and smile. We therefore decided it was an appropriate placement. Baby G had found her home.

Chapter 8:

IDENTITY CRISIS-THE TURNING POINT

When I recount my early professional experience, I realize I was progressing nicely in that arena, but at the same time I was searching for my personal identity.

The identity issues I faced in my twenties were not unlike those confronted by young adults of other generations. In Erik Erikson's developmental terms, I was establishing fidelity to ideals, religious values, friendship, and love relationships. My efforts to deal with those issues in the maturational upheaval of young adulthood were complicated by my own particular intra-psychic conflicts and culminated in an emotional break-down, replete with psychosomatic symptoms and depression. I emerged from my identity crisis with increased awareness of my conflict about marriage vs. career, but it was not until later that I realized I had chosen my work instead of marriage.

I found living on my own exciting and felt confident I could take care of myself and my essential material needs. I assumed I would marry and have a home of my own someday and could make do until then. My salary in Richmond was

not much more than the one hundred twenty five dollars per
month that I received in Fauquier County, but an automobile
was furnished for my work. I sold my pre-war, 1939
Oldsmobile back to the veteran from whom I had bought it.
The sale provided me the financial margin I needed to live in
the city.

My financial resources were pinched but my standard of
living was comparable to that of other unmarried young people I knew. I managed my limited resources well, made most
of my clothes, shared apartments or lived in rooming houses.
My living quarters were decorated Bohemian-style with
orange crates and burlap, dripping candles, and fine art
prints. The idea of owning an automobile was simply out of
the question. I resented the time it took, but riding the bus
was a fact of life. It seemed to me that I had never had as
much money before for entertainment, clothing, and special
treats. I even saved a little money at the same time I was pay-
ing off my college loans.

Finding my way socially and making new friends was
much more demanding than establishing my independence.
When I went to Richmond, I first lived in a rooming house
on Monument Avenue. I arrived with my suitcase and a box
of Virginia sugar cured ham and biscuits from home, and
soon cultivated new acquaintances, who became friends.
Gracious candlelight dinners at the Tearoom next door balanced the inconvenience of sharing the bath down the hall
with a half dozen others. The dinner hour, at least, was remi-
niscent of the gracious way of life Mary Washington had
promised. Most of us, who lived in the rooming house,
worked at or near the Medical College of Virginia, which was
located across the street from my office.

Ellen Gilmer, a social worker who worked with me, and I
became close friends and shared our first apartment with Ann
Jordan, a medical secretary, whom I knew from the rooming
house. We were all recent college graduates and shared many
interests in common. Ellen had graduated from Randolph

Macon Woman's college in Lynchburg and Ann from Mary Baldwin in Staunton. We entertained our boyfriends, in the hot summer of 1946, with suppers of Virginia sugar cured ham and fried green apples that Ann's father had brought us from Staunton.

Forming relationships of some depth with friends, old and new, male and female, single and married, was an important part of my experience in living on my own. I don't think I recognized then how essential my friends' support and validation was to me.

Some of my friends viewed me as more sophisticated than I was. I tried to conceal my naiveté and lack of experience. I desperately wanted to feel connected, to carry my share of the responsibility in relationships, but I often felt anxious about whether I knew the right thing to do or say. I had much catching up to do, much I had not appropriately learned in adolescence. In my personal sphere, I still viewed the world as a safe and friendly place with no danger, harm or evil. I missed the fun I might have had if I had felt more comfortable about myself in my interaction with others. Feelings of alienation and depression sometimes interfered with my spontaneity.

My boundless idealism and faith in human nature fit with the idealism of the post-war period. I wanted peace as much as the rest of the world. Belief in the four freedoms incorporated in the United Nations Charter became as much a part of me as breathing. Men and women had died for those freedoms; living for them had new meaning. My discovery of social conditions in my home community and in the State of Virginia required a reappraisal of my Southern roots and culture.

I searched for ways to live out my ideals in my civic, religious, and professional activities. Elizabeth Seay, a social worker and friend in Richmond, encouraged me to become active in the United World Federalists, an organization that supported the ideals of the United Nations. I learned about social action from Paul Keve, a social worker who was also a probation officer, when I appeared before the Virginia State

Legislature on behalf of delinquent adolescents. I shopped around for a church, worshipped with the Friends and the Unitarians, and joined Grace Presbyterian Church, which had an active, socially conscious youth group.

When I moved to Arlington I found the church that I was looking for, and, along with friends, attended All Souls Unitarian Church in Washington, D.C. At that time, A. Powell Davies, D.D., the minister, was well known as a social activist and a leading theologian. In Arlington, I joined the Association of University Women and the Junior Women's Club, of which I soon became president. I was also active in professional organizations.

Some of my friends viewed my bravado for approaching changes in the world as inappropriate for a woman. They looked upon my involvement in social work with amusement, pointedly ignoring whatever I had to say. Male friends enjoyed taking me to task about my idealistic convictions. I think it was because my response was more authentically lively than my characteristic passive demure demeanor. My Uncle Bill, a Baptist minister, and I argued about my changing religious views. My Uncle Forrest tried to persuade me to go to medical school and be a doctor if I wanted to help people. My parents often said they wished I had chosen a more genteel profession, such as teaching, and expressed their concern about my exposure to the world's sordidness and pain.

Establishing my fidelity to ideals seemed clear in my thinking compared to some of the other issues. My womanhood and sexuality could not be ignored, but my feelings about them were befuddled. My need for connection with others was an important part of my effort to form love relationships with men, but my unconscious fears of intimacy and loss stood in the way.

I assumed I would be chosen for marriage with little participation on my part. I would just look pretty, smile sweetly, and say yes or no when the time came. "Nice young ladies are recognized, sought out," was a part of the Southern culture. I was sought out by many fine young men, good friends, with whom I had corresponded during the war, and who were returning in 1945 and 1946, I often said no, but never a wholehearted yes.

In 1946, Bill, the brother of a Mary Washington friend, whose family had sent me flowers on his behalf while he was overseas, returned and proposed on Easter weekend, when I was invited to visit his family in Richmond. Andy, an engineer, who had invited me to Virginia Polytechnic Institute for football weekends and big band dances, and visited me at Mary Washington, gave me one last chance before marrying a nurse he knew in Europe. Henry, who was back from the Pacific and in medical school, visited me at my family's home and invited me to visit his family in Michigan.

In my visit to Henry's home, his mother entertained at luncheons and parties in my honor, and introduced me to their extended family, thinking ours was a serious romance. Henry took me to a poker party where I stood out like a sore thumb among his friends. I didn't know one card from another. I withdrew. Henry wrote, in his next letter, that his mother thought I was "a very practical young lady" and that he was in love with someone else. I was disappointed, as we had corresponded weekly for four years and all the externals for a good marriage were there. He was bright, interesting, and studying to be a doctor. I liked his parents as much as they apparently liked me. Henry's rejection posed questions for me: was it because I refused to have sex, or because I was so unsophisticated, or because my heart wasn't in it?

My parents tried to counsel me that it was marriage time. They graciously extended their hospitality to my male friends and made it their business to ascertain or assess their honorable intentions. The problem was that the young men who returned from war were ready to get married and made it clear that a diamond engagement ring was contingent upon a sexual response and/or commitment from me. I told myself I was in love with Joe, the soldier from Vint Hill who had not yet returned from overseas. It is now clear to me that I was not ready to make a commitment, but I was not in touch with that then.

In the summer of 1950, when I returned home to Fauquier County on a temporary leave of absence from my work in Arlington, before I attended graduate school, I was aware of an overwhelming sense of sadness and despair that I attributed to a broken heart. Joe had reappeared in my life but, once more, disappeared. For the first time, I had known the joy and excitement of a mutually reciprocal attraction and romantic relationship with a man. Many years later, I learned Joe saw me as a powerful and independent woman who chose career. I had not dared to let him know how much I cared. I also realized later that it was I, not he, who had sabotaged our relationship by finding ways to distance.

Since identity crises are usually precipitated by extraneous events that touch upon vulnerable areas, I think a cumulative series of losses or perceived losses were precipitating factors at that time. The loss of my family's home by fire a year after I left home to work in Richmond was a major trauma. My brother, who was returning from the Navy, and I were pulled back into the family before we had an opportunity to become firmly established on our own. We needed to help our parents. We wanted to help, but the trauma took its toll on both our lives.

In 1948, my grandmother Updike, to whom I was deeply attached, became terminally ill and died. I felt sad but I could not bear to visit her or even attend her funeral. My brother and his wife were secretly married in June of that year, when he was twenty-one and she was seventeen. Because her mother had asked me to chaperone them while she was out of town, I tried to obstruct their plans to get married. My well-intentioned effort was a serious blunder. They never forgave me and I felt I lost the closeness I had previously enjoyed with my brother.

At the time of my breakdown, in the summer of 1950, I

wandered barefoot through the fields of home, rode horse-back, renewed old friendships, made new friends, and thought I could be perfectly content to remain in Fauquier County for the rest of my life. But it was not to be. Heinz Hartman's, "Regression in the service of the ego" accurately captures the state I was in and my recovery back home prior to leaving for graduate school.

The New York School of Social Work turned down my application when I, ever the idealist, told the truth about my emotional state in an autobiographical statement. When my mother realized I was about to marry a farmer on the re-bound, she pushed me to apply to other schools of social work. My child welfare fellowship had already been granted contingent upon my acceptance by a social work school.

By October 1950, two other schools of social work had accepted my application, and I was working again, temporarily, at the Fauquier County Welfare Department for Lina Cameron and living in Warrenton. I remember my agonizing hours of decision that fall. Walking down Main Street, from the welfare office to Dr. and Mrs. Trow's home, where I was boarding, I would creep into the warmth of the candlelight in the Catholic Church and meditate and pray. Was my commitment to child welfare and professional training holding or was I to remain in Fauquier County indefinitely?

As the feminist I was at heart, I didn't comprehend or accept the necessity to make a choice between marriage and career. The men I was interested in did not agree with my perspective. After crying at one more wedding because it wasn't mine, and a serious bout with pneumonia, I was off to St. Louis for my first year of graduate training in January 1951. Following my first year of training, I worked another year in Arlington before completing the work for my M.S.W. (Masters of Social Work) at the New York School of Social Work, Columbia University.

Chapter 9:

PROFESSIONAL TRAINING AND PSYCHOANALYSIS

At a look back upon my graduate training and my psychoanalysis, I think each was a transformative experience, both personally and professionally. Graduate training in two schools of social work helped me to winnow the grain from the chaff of what I had learned in my child welfare experience and to sharpen and expand my skills. I found the opportunity to explore what I wanted to learn tremendously exciting. I felt fortunate to attend these two schools in different parts of the country, and I valued the balanced perspective their differences gave me. My psychoanalysis with a Sullivanian analyst shook me loose from my roots and freed me to grow again.

Although I had taken part-time graduate courses at three schools: Richmond, the National Catholic School of Social Service, and the New York School of Social Work, my first year of full-time graduate training was at the George Warren Brown School of Social Work at Washington University in St. Louis, Missouri in 1951. My second year was at the New York School of Social Work, Columbia University in 1952 and 1953.

The curriculum in accredited schools of social work in the early fifties was generic. Students were expected to develop a working familiarity with the basic methods of social work as a foundation for practice in any field. The methods courses required for all students included social casework, social group work, community organization, social welfare administration, and research.

My choice of psychiatric social work as a specialization and my commitment to child welfare practice led me to choose field work placements in a children's residential treatment center for emotionally disturbed children in St. Louis, and a child guidance clinic in Brooklyn. At that time, child guidance clinics were well established and children's treatment institutions for emotionally disturbed children were beginning to replace orphanages. I promised myself I would take what I learned about psychotherapy with children and their parents back to child welfare when I returned to Arlington, and I did. Throughout my career, whenever I worked with adults, my empathic imagination was fueled by trying to visualize what the childhood experience of the person or persons before me might have been like.

The Department of Social Work was established in the School of Business and Public Administration at Washington University in 1925. The George Warren Brown School of Social Work became a separate school at Washington University in 1945-1946.

Dean Benjamin Youngdahl welcomed me warmly on an icy morning in January 1951. I had flown to Chicago and then to St. Louis in a snow storm the night before and had spent a sleepless night at the YWCA. That was my first experience flying. St. Louis was strange to me and I felt anxious. I wanted to be sure I was at the school on time for registration and so arrived before the school opened.

The George Warren Brown School of Social Work building was a handsome structure designed to fit with the college

Gothic architecture of Washington University. None of my social work quarters before had prepared me for the comfort and luxury of this setting, aesthetically pleasing and conducive to study and socialization with other students.

Most of my classmates were from the Midwest or Far West. Our class was small; the intimacy of our inter-personal exchange in learning was heightened by an accelerated plan for the first year of graduate training.

Twyla Boe, from South Dakota, and I walked to the cafeteria and classes together. We enjoyed comparing our child welfare experiences in Virginia and South Dakota, and our early upbringing on farms in those two states. Arlene Patterson, from Ohio, who also had her fieldwork placement in a children's treatment institution, became a friend for life.

My fieldwork placement in a treatment institution for emotionally disturbed children was an exceptional learning experience, though one not without problems. My supervisor was a skilled clinician who had worked at the Jewish Board of Guardians in New York. He considered my view of my casework skills as inflated and was challenged to change my view of myself as a woman. I learned a lot about institutional care and began learning about psychotherapy, using what I knew about working with children. I worked with six emotionally disturbed girls between the ages of nine and sixteen. Alice Mulholm, another Smith School of Social Work graduate, who was my faculty advisor, guided me through the difficult placement.

The stimulation of the academic setting served me well. My performance at George Warren Brown was outstanding, and I re-submitted my application to the New York School of Social Work for my second year of graduate training. I was accepted for graduate training for the 1952-53 academic year.

A young colleague in a study group recently told me she would consider it a privilege to know the "old-time psychiatric social workers" who were trained at Smith or the New York School of Social Work. I was reminded that I am one of those old time psychiatric social workers, and that the training I received in the 50s, prepared me for my career path in the last half of the twentieth century as well.

I am proud of my social work heritage, which has maintained the image of Jane Addams working in the tenement houses of Chicago at the turn of the last century, and Mary Richmond, who first defined social casework in the 1930s.

Following the only visit of Sigmund Freud to America, in 1909, on which he was accompanied by his colleague, Carl Jung, psychoanalytic ideas became a pervasive influence on twentieth century thought. In the thirties, while public agencies were focusing on meeting economic needs, new relationships were developing with psychiatry. Child guidance clinics offered consultation to agency workers. Some social agencies, particularly childrens' agencies and family agencies, sought consultation and arranged for staff seminars with private psychoanalysts. This collaboration became increasingly popular, particularly, in military clinical settings during the war and, eventually, in public agencies.

The New York School of Social Work offered the first formal courses in social work in the United States in 1898. The celebration of the centennial, which was celebrated throughout the United States in June 1998, refreshed my recollection of my experience in New York. Gordon Hamilton, a leader in the field of social work, was the Dean of the school. Lucille Austin and Florence Hollis, well known for their contribution to casework theory, were among my favorite teachers.

Casework was still considered a major part of the curriculum for all students—casework with a psychoanalytic bent. Rivalry was intense for Lucille Austin's class. She was an attractive and exciting person, a scintillating teacher who drew out the best thinking and experience of every student. Her intellect and her charm made her class a special experience. Once, I recall, we pressed her for an answer as to why the New York School was psychoanalytically oriented. Her response was that the school viewed it as essential that we master one

theoretical view from which we could explore others in practice. I realized only later that the New York School's approach
and the psychoanalytical orientation were synonymous.

Florence Hollis, whose writing on the casework relationship was widely recognized, was my thesis advisor. She helped
me to design my research project and think through the
methodology and conclusions. "Casework Skills and
Techniques Used in the Treatment of the Compulsive Mother
in the Child Guidance Clinic" was the subject of my project
and the title of my Master's thesis. I studied more than a hundred case records at the Bureau of Child Guidance, Brooklyn
Board of Education, where I had my field work, and chose ten
to explore more carefully. I identified casework skills and techniques and charted them on rolls of butcher paper that seemed
to be miles long. My findings were strikingly different from the
literature of the day. Florence Hollis encouraged me to publish
my results, which I never did. My conclusion, in essence, was
that the casework relationship was more important than the
skills and techniques used by the caseworker.

Many years later, in 1985, I had the pleasure of hearing
Florence Hollis speak on the West Coast at Stanford
University. I realized that in some small way, I had contributed
to her research and writing on the casework relationship and
that the conclusion I reached in my research project had been
a basic tenet of my practice throughout my career. One of the
last persons I saw in my private practice forty years later had
once been diagnosed as a compulsive mother in a child guidance clinic. My thesis conclusions, that the casework relationship was more important than the skills and techniques used,
still held.

The last course I took at the New York School in 1953 was
a seminar in social work with Nathan Cohen, Ph.D., Associate
Dean, one of the earliest practitioners of community organization and group work. The seminar's aim was the integration
of the different mehods of the generic curriculum. The learning process was sizzling!

I remember that as he talked about Robert Moses, the power broker of New York City, I thought of every experience I had ever had that remotely resembled community organization. In Richmond, Paul Keve, a probation officer, had introduced me to social action on behalf of delinquent children with the Virginia State Legislature. In St. Louis, at George Warren Brown, Helen Hayden, a professor, had taken our community organization class to Kansas City to the state legislature on a field trip. I had organized foster mothers in Arlington for the purpose of achieving training for their job as foster parents. And, before my graduate training, I had organized a community center in the vacant schoolhouse in Orlean. I remembered that even before I knew of Jane Addams I was following my mother around in the thirties to organize a WPA class for people who were illiterate. It was all coming together. Even though psychiatric social work was my special interest, community organization and social action was to become part of my professional and personal way of life.

◎　◎　◎　◎　◎

I think of the year I was in New York as the peak experience of my early adulthood, academically and personally. The New York School of Social Work was located in the old Carnegie Mansion, now the Cooper Hewitt National Museum of Design on East 91st Street at 5th Avenue. I walked to school, window shopped on 5th Avenue, and thoroughly enjoyed Central Park and the Metropolitan Museum of Art located nearby.

Three of us students, including my friend, Kathryn Lee from Arlington, subleased a designer decorated railroad flat on East 89th Street, near Gracie Mansion, the mayor's residence on the East Side. We later learned that we were living in a slum that was in a famous sociological study. We thought our quarters were luxurious. We had eight rooms, including a music room with a grand piano, for $90 per month. I lived on my fellowship money, $100 dollars a month, including my third of the rent. We got acquainted with a butcher in Yorkville, who saved us good bones for soup; we ate onion and rye bread sandwiches, sometimes with cheese. I felt handsomely attired. I had a new red tweed suit that I purchased from Saks Fifth Avenue with money my parents gave me to buy new clothes, and a wardrobe I had made for myself before I left Arlington, which included linen blouses and a black faille dress. I still keep a rhinestone costume jewelry pin I bought to set off that black dress.

I had visited New York frequently when I lived in Arlington. It was the most exciting place I knew. The autumn was brisk and colorful, snowfall in winter was magical. I loved the rush. I couldn't get enough of riding the subway, whether for my fieldwork in Brooklyn or to see the dawn in Manhattan, after all night student parties in Greenwich Village.

Standing room for opera tickets, Broadway plays, and art museums provided entertainment. And not to miss a romantic beat, I was having my first affair with a French artist. I felt good about myself as a woman and excited to be alive.

◉   ◉   ◉   ◉   ◉

Psychoanalysis was a part of the popular culture as well as the academic culture of which I was a part in the 40s and 50s. In graduate school, I saw that it was desirable, if not necessary, for one's professional development. I was strongly motivated to seek psychoanalytic therapy at my earliest opportunity. Soon I found psychotherapy was as essential to me personally as it was to my professional development.

My psychoanalysis is a part of my development without which the story of my life and career would not be complete. I do not intend to describe it in detail. I respect my privacy as I respect the privacy of others. But I think it is important to share some of the meaning it has had for me and some of the lessons I am still learning from it.

When I returned to Arlington, after completing my graduate training in June 1953, I met a young Washington attorney, whose active pursuit of me, was what I had expected should precede marriage. That summer I started furnishing my first apartment. We found we had many interests in common. We played tennis, canoed on the Potomac, hiked, learned to tango, were active in the Unitarian Church, and visited my family and friends in Fauquier County. He was a very demanding person who wouldn't let me out of his sight. Our wills clashed, particularly on the subject of how much time I would spend on my work and how much with him. By the end of the year, the prospect of marriage was becoming a pressure that I had trouble coping with, in addition to my new supervisory job.

I think, as is true for most persons who seek psychotherapy or psychoanalysis, the distress of unbearable personal discomfort and anxiety precipitated my urgent request for help.

Fortunately, the doors opened immediately. Leslie Farber, M.D., who had recently arrived in Washington from San Francisco, offered me an appointment for the next day. He had studied at the old Baltimore-Washington Psychoanalytic Institute under Harry Stack Sullivan, and was a training and supervisory psychoanalyst at the Washington Psychoanalytic Institute. I remember getting a yes and no answer when I inquired if he was a Freudian psychoanalyst. That was very important to me at the time since I had just graduated from the New York School of Social Work.

But Dr. Farber's background and theoretical orientation did not seem as important to me as his willingness to see me immediately. I felt I made a connection in the first hour. We worked out an agreement to meet four times a week for a reduced rate of $350 a month, which was more than half of my take-home pay. Later, I understood he gave me a reduced rate, as a professional courtesy, because I was a social worker.

I was sufficiently familiar with psychoanalytic terminology by 1953 when I finished graduate school that I had a label for any piece of my behavior or others' behavior. One of Dr. Farber's few stated rules of psychotherapy was that I must use plain language, "no terminology" to describe what I was talking about. Breaking the silence to begin those hours was one of the most difficult experiences I can remember. I shall never forget the light and movement in a painting I watched on his wall.

The only intervention I recall Dr. Farber making was when my attorney friend was pressuring me for a commitment. Dr. Farber suggested I ask him, "Are you willing to take the responsibility for my mental health?" My friend disappeared but returned a year later to present a formal plan for our engagement and marriage. We had had dinner and were dancing on the terrace at the Shoreham Hotel. I upset the apple cart by suggesting we get married immediately. My "Why not now?" shocked him out of town again, forever. He thought I was viewing his proposal lightly, and perhaps I was. I think it was the right choice for both of us, although I have always felt badly about the hurt it caused him.

Once I had learned in therapy to assess what I wanted in life, there was still the problem of being in touch with what I didn't want. It seems strange now to recall that one of the most important things I got from my psychoanalysis was a deeper appreciation of aesthetics—music, art, literature, nature. I remember being ecstatic about nature and enthralled that a man I met liked to garden, only to discover later that I didn't like the man.

Some of the things I learned from my psychoanalysis with Dr. Farber were:

- Communication is a two way street; neither therapists and patients, nor husbands and wives, nor parents and children, nor any one person and another can know for sure what the other is thinking and feeling without the spoken word.

- Learning to know what one wants in life is essential to choice. Choice is required. Will is ours to use, not to hide.
- Finding one's way is necessary for individuation.
- The genuineness of human emotion and emotional exchange is a part of intimacy.
- Authenticity is being there, being who and what you are.
- Love is what you give, not just what you get.
- The search for beauty in nature, art, music, life needs to be intentional.
- Use of one's talents in the simplest endeavors— cooking, sewing, decorating, and gardening—and in one's profession is creativity.
- The spiritual search is a continuous one.
- The search for self-understanding continues as long as one lives.

Dr. Farber brought Martin Buber, the famous Jewish theologian and philosopher, to this country, and was influenced by Buber's I/Thou principle and so was I.

Although we worked through a plan for termination before I made plans to move to the west coast, I saw Dr. Farber for a check-up before I left and several times thereafter. The first time was when I went back east after my father died and later, when I planned to be married.

When I read the obituary notice of Dr. Farber's death, twenty-five years later, I felt fresh, pure, strong feelings of grief. I thought I had never dealt with these feelings in my analysis. But it was clear they were accessible.

The gold beaded cloche I wore for my employment interview at Langley Porter Neuropsychiatric Institute

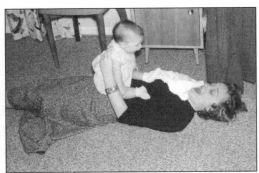

Enjoying travel and friend's children

IV. THE JOURNEY

1956-1979

Herrick Hospital, where I went to work at Herrick-City of Berkeley
Outpatient Psychiatric Clinic

Merle and Bob, Chuck, age 13 and Jennifer, age 5
Career and Family Life Converge

Chapter 10:

FINDING THE STILL POINT

Langley Porter Neuropsychiatric Institute
San Francisco, California, 1956-62

While I didn't know it at the time, my next move was permanent. The journey began in November 1956, when I traveled across the country from the East Coast to California.

For the first five and a half years I lived in San Francisco
and worked at Langley Porter Neuropsychiatric Institute,
which was then known as one of the finest psychiatric training and research centers west of the Mississippi.

A "shadow," as the Jungian's say, follows me from those
years that is both bright and vibrant and dark and treacherous.
As I look back at it, the grace of God held me in the eye of the
storm until I could find my center, a still point between east
and west, past and future, self and others.

My decision to move to California was my choice. No one
invited, recruited, or sought me out. Everyone I knew seemed
shocked that I was so clear about what I wanted.

But I thought, *why not?* My obligation for my fellowship was completed; my loans for college and graduate school were paid. My analyst and I agreed that we had done our work. The world and my place in it seemed harmonious. I was ready to choose where I could work to get the clinical experience I knew I needed.

My friends questioned my making this move. Harvey and Dorcas in Fauquier County simply couldn't understand how I could leave Virginia, "the most beautiful place on earth." Arlene and Pat, friends in Annapolis, tried to remain neutral even though they questioned my judgment. Ruth, my best friend since college days, saw it as an avant-garde move for a single woman in the 50s. She envied my career as I envied her role as a wife and mother.

My parents grieved, thinking of relatives who had gone west and never returned. They comprehended, more fully than I did, that I was separating from home and family.

My colleagues at the Arlington Welfare Department, wished me well with a full set of Samsonite luggage, knowing that my mind was made up, that it was time for me to pursue the career in psychiatric social work for which I had prepared in graduate school.

My feelings of sadness at leaving my friends and family were overcome by the excitement of adventure, seeing new sights, exploring new possibilities. I wanted to leave the crowded, sultry East Coast for wide-open spaces.

I recall feeling deep concern about the conflict I saw arising from the integration of schools in Virginia. Robert Cullers, my cousin, a bright young journalist, was disinherited because of the stand he took to support integration in the Front Royal public schools. He wrote a letter to the Editor of *The Warren Sentinel*, his hometown newspaper, making his views public. Even though Thomas Wolfe's, *You Can't Go Home Again*, stirred my emotions deeply, I had no sense of the conflict I would experience for the rest of my life about leaving the south.

California captivated my imagination. A friend, Jim, had written me about his recent experiences crossing the Continental Divide, finding an exciting new job in San Diego, living in La Jolla, and surfing in the Pacific. He also sent information about jobs that I might pursue. Marianne Rousseau, who was a clever, stylish, sophisticate on the Washington, D.C. cocktail party circuit, had left for California as bored with the Washington scene as I had become and was already married in less than a year. She was a medical social worker, a Smith graduate, who had found a lucrative new job in public health in San Francisco. She told me social workers trained in the East were highly valued on the West Coast. Betty and Bill Snyder, my close relatives, who were in the Navy, would welcome my visits in Coronado, near San Diego. Minto and Harry Keaton, friends from Berkeley, California, whom I had known in Arlington, were now in Los Angeles. What more did I need for contacts on the West Coast?

When I closed my apartment in Arlington, gave away most of my furniture, packed a trunk to send express, and took off with my new set of luggage, it was not my conscious intent to make a lasting move to the West Coast. Often, I have looked back to see if I could discern the marker for my permanency in California. When was it clear that I had come to stay? Perhaps before I started.

In looking over my personnel file, I found that I had thoroughly explored other options. There was a job offer from a child guidance clinic in Winnetka, Illinois; encouraging correspondence from the Jewish Board of Guardians in New York City about a job in a children's treatment institution; a U.S. Government contract I had never signed for a top administrative position in mental health in the Panama Canal Zone I also found, in that file, copies of applications that I had sent to California for Senior Psychiatric Social Worker (P.S.W.) positions. I had taken and passed the oral examination for the California Department of Mental Hygiene, Senior P.S.W. position, the week before I left.

Taking the oral examination was one reason I left from New York. Another was that I wanted one last look at this city I so loved; I wanted to compare it with San Francisco, which I had heard was the next most exciting city in the country. I also wanted the support of my friends, Ruth and Frank Kluge, who lived in Westchester County. Their home was, and still is, "my home to come home to" emotionally.

Ruth and Frank and I were friends since Mary Washington College days when we sent Frank, who was in the Coast Guard, off to D-Day. I attended their wedding in 1945. I was with them and Ruth's family in Westchester County, New York, on the night in 1946, when I learned by telephone that my parents' home had burned down and my family was incommunicado. I visited the Kluges frequently when I was at the New York School of Social Work and while I was working in Arlington. I was fond of their three children, Lynn, Steven, and Mary Ellen. I knew I would miss my visits with them. I see the Kluges, and friends like them, as the safety net that protected me in some of my most vulnerable years, while I was living on both coasts.

My friend, Mary Anne Rousseau and her new husband, Frank Grady, met me at the Oakland Airport after what seemed like an interminable flight across the country. On my first night in California, they took me to Nob Hill to see San Francisco. They entertained and supported me in their first home in the Marina District, while I stumbled about in finding a job and a place to live other than the Y.W.C.A. I thought I had never seen such illumination as the light bouncing off their white walls on to their paintings and brightly-colored oriental rugs on their floors. I was amazed when Frank, wearing an apron, cooked dinner. I had never seen a man do that before.

In searching for a job, I went first for an interview at the Napa State Mental Hospital, and had a gut-level discomfort at the idea of being a part of that enormous institution. That recognition surprised me since I had visited big mental hospitals in Richmond, St. Louis and New York City.

Upon my return from Napa to San Francisco, I found a warm welcoming message from Helen Byron, Chief P.S.W., at Langley Porter Neuropsychiatric Institute. She invited me for a preliminary interview. I was becoming a little apprehensive as my money was running out after less than a week in California.

I was a sitting duck paradox as I approached that interview, so sure of my qualifications and myself and so insecure at the same time. My first permanent had left my hair frizzy. The sales person at I. Magnin, one of San Francisco's large department stores, saved me. At her suggestion, I bought a striking red and black, layered cloche hat with gold beads to cover the frizz and to set off the heavy, dull, gray striped wool dress I had tailored myself before I left the east. Little did I know then, as I learned years later, that my appearance was viewed as "sensational" by the psychiatric staff and residents when I arrived at Langley Porter.

Helen Byron was sensitive, direct, and engaging in her interviewing skills and I soon saw that here was the exciting opportunity I was looking for. She evidently confirmed her impression from my written application that I was the one for the job and arranged for a follow-up interview with Alexander Simon, M.D., director, Cloyce Duncan, M.D., chief of inpatient service and John Guerrant, M.D., head of M3 and W3, the men's and women's wards on which I would be working. After a tour of the inpatient service, and their careful observations of my reactions to locked wards, patients, and staff, I was offered the job.

As Chief P.S.W. and my supervisor, Helen Byron took on the role as my mentor throughout our working relationship. She advised me about the complex administrative structure, inter-disciplinary relationships, and policy issues, as well as about new experiences I could expect to encounter in San Francisco, such as excessive use of alcohol, homosexuality, and sexual approaches by married man.

Langley Porter was a new earthquake-resistant, concrete four-story building built in 1942 at Arguello and Parnassus Avenues, by the Department of Mental Hygiene. It was next door to the University of California Medical Center, to which it was linked administratively. Located on Parnassus Heights, near the Pacific Ocean and the Golden Gate Park, and over-looking the Golden Gate, it was a cold setting, inside and out. I wore my wool suit and sweater and Harris tweed coat all year, as I was not used to the fog and the chill.

My office, at the back of a locked women's ward, was con-sidered a prize location and envied by staff. But I saw it as a large cubicle of concrete, with a small window facing eucalyp-tus trees, a bleak habitat, in which I never was so lonely and spent as little time as possible.

A first-year psychiatric resident was soon dropping by to cheer me. We got to be good friends at work. Trying to main-tain my professional demeanor, I made an effort to keep the professional boundaries clear. I recall some pleasant breaks in the routine though—windy walks around Parnassus Heights in back of the Hospital, chats about skiing, and quite by chance, it seemed, rides home from the Unitarian Church, which we both attended. He was my kind of guy—friendly, outgoing, easy to be with, and even had a Southern accent. But I was frozen in my tracks, telling myself I would wait to become more personally friendly until the appropriate time, when he had finished his first year of training on M3 and W4. By then he was engaged to a nurse, and I had found a rela-tionship with someone who had no connection with Langley Porter. It was no wonder I was wary in my relationships with psychiatric residents and staff. While I was in graduate school, I had the experience in which under the guise of learning about transference and counter-transference, I was sexually harassed.

I was overwhelmed by the complexity of the administra-tive structure, the interdisciplinary collaboration, the excite-ment of the learning opportunity and the outstanding leader-

ship and competence of my social work colleagues. Some of
the other social workers seemed particularly adept at not
showing their feelings, so I thought I needed to wear a professional masque too. I missed the camaraderie and informality
of my child welfare days.

The stress and tension of working in the psychiatric setting at Langley Porter was hard. I soon learned that every
interpersonal exchange; every interaction was grist for the
mill. No word went unexamined by staff.

Schizophrenia was the predominant research focus.
Gregory Bateson, Jurgen Reusch, and others at Langley Porter,
were widely known for their contributions to research in communication theory. It sometimes seemed to me that every
patient, whose case was presented in clinical conferences, had a
diagnosis of schizophrenia. A great deal of investigation was
going on about the use of psychotropic medication.

But persons with diagnoses other than schizophrenia were
admitted for instructional purposes—as were persons from
different racial, cultural and economic backgrounds, and persons from different developmental levels—adolescence, young
adulthood, mid-life, older adulthood. Severely disturbed or
suicidally depressed persons, who were public figures, celebri-
ties, artists, musicians, professionals, were admitted under
political pressure. All admissions were voluntary and patients
and their families were charged fees according to their ability
to pay. Most patients were admitted for longer-term treatment, ranging from at least six months to a year or more, and
some patients, particularly adolescents and young adults, were
hospitalized for two or three years.

Admission to Langley Porter was widely sought by people
in Northern California. Among ourselves, staff and trainees,
we referred to it as the Chestnut Lodge of the West (Chestnut
Lodge was a well-known private psychiatric hospital near
Washington, D.C.). For many years, I would consider it my
hospital of choice if anyone I loved should need psychiatric
hospitalization.

The family was the focus of my clinical work. I maintained continuous contact with family members from admission to discharge, helping them understand patients' progress, preparing them for home visits and discharge. Psychotherapy with family members was part of every treatment plan. Their willingness to participate in therapy was a requirement of admission.

Langley Porter's Children's Service was widely known for working with the family as the unit of treatment, and the concept was used as a model by the adult inpatient service. We called it "collaborative therapy" before the introduction of the term "family therapy" at the Mental Research Institute in Palo Alto. As family therapy became more accepted, we moved increasingly in that direction. Lois Cammack Bateson, another social worker on the inpatient service, and I took training at the Mental Research Institute with Virginia Satir. We were really out front with family therapy, but in our research mode at Langley Porter, "Hid our light under a bushel."

I remember the parents of a brilliant eighteen-year-old college freshman who was diagnosed with schizophrenia. They drove 500 miles every week for more than two years for separate interviews with a resident and me, and a family therapy interview with the patient, two residents, and myself. These parents were devoted, responsible, caring, and broken-hearted. Once, many years later, I ran into them by chance and learned their son had made a reasonably satisfactory adjustment to the world, and they thought their effort in psychotherapy and family therapy was worthwhile.

Mostly I worked with families of adolescents. I remember, particularly, working with a mother who traveled 300 miles on the bus for her interview with me every week for three years. She once brought me a suit box filled with camellias. I thought they were the most beautiful flowers I had ever seen. This was before I learned that taking a gift was taboo. Even after I knew better, I honored the culture of my client rather than professional protocol, when a mother who owned a gift shop in Chinatown, insisted upon giving me a tea cozy. I still cherish that gift as a reminder of my Langley Porter days.

Teaching social work concepts and the use of social work services to psychiatric residents and trainees of other disciplines was a major part of my responsibilities. My observations and thinking about patient care were valued by staff, often welcomed, but sometimes begrudgingly tolerated, by psychiatric residents. The interdisciplinary challenge was to learn to collaborate in developing and modifying diagnostic formulations and treatment plans.

While I had a close identification with members of the psychiatric social work staff, I functioned in relative isolation from other P.S.W.'s. Administratively, I was responsible to both Helen Byron, the Chief P.S.W., and to the staff psychiatrist in charge of the two-inpatient wards and had weekly supervisory conferences with each of them. My professional identity seemed to waver between my identification with social work, my profession, and psychiatry.

Before I left Langley Porter, I became aware of conflict in the system when social workers were made responsible to psychiatrists. But it was not until later, I realized this was a historical turning point in the struggle our profession has had in maintaining its identity. For it was then, Bob Dean, a P.S.W., on the teaching staff at the University of California Medical Center, took leadership in the establishment of clinical social work and licensing for clinical social workers.

I did not know the details then, but when I was writing this book thirty-six years later, I interviewed Helen Byron, who at ninety-three recalled clearly the struggle my profession had maintaining its separate identity in an inter-disciplinary setting. She told me that she had been disappointed and disillusioned that the National Association of Social Work (NASW) had not supported her in the conflict. She had strongly supported Bob Dean in his leadership for licensing of clinical social workers. Rewriting my own professional identity has made my identity as a social worker, a psychiatric social worker, and a clinical social worker clearer.

The lessons I learned at Langley Porter established a solid base for the development of my clinical skills. I learned a great deal about differential diagnosis and treatment, management of suicidal and violent behavior, the complex administrative structure, and the effect of conflict on staff and patients as it reverberated throughout the system.

◎   ◎   ◎   ◎   ◎

My personal development in those years, my thirties, was turbulent. My psyche was in a state of flux that was continuously stirred up by the intensity of my work environment in a psychiatric training center and the stimulation of living in San Francisco. I was challenged to use my insights from psychoanalysis but I soon learned, as I know even better today, that insight does not always translate into more effective behavior. My yearning for connection, for relationship, and my growing independence was a painful conflict that often led to loneliness and depression. I wanted a life of my own, and the mutuality of a relationship, but I found that most of the men I got to know were even more skilled than I was at keeping a safe distance.

The beauty and excitement of living in San Francisco will always be a favorite memory. The City entranced me as it captures most visitors with the sight of its hills—Nob Hill, Telegraph Hill, Russian Hill—its steep streets, its clear air, and its sunlit, azure waters. I thought the bay window was invented so that everyone could have a view, whether from its old Victorian houses called "painted ladies" or apartment buildings. Looking upon it as the "alabaster city" from Marin County across the Golden Gate Bridge was like a dream. The fog creeping in and the sound of the foghorns at night soothed my restless spirit. The scene of the Pacific Ocean, the scent of the eucalyptus trees, from the steep, winding curves on Route One in Marin County, the fog-cleansed air, was an entirely new experience. Muir Woods, Mt. Tamalpais, Stinson

Beach provided memorable day trips. Sailing across the bay to Sausalito and Tiburon was exciting.

For the first six months I was in San Francisco, I lived in Pacific Heights, on Octavia Street, in the Lafayette Residence Club, which had once been a famous old mansion with a handsome winding stairway and pink marble bathrooms. An unwritten code that men and women who lived there would not date one another resulted in group outings, and platonic friendships that lasted for many years. Later, I dated several of the men I knew there, but these relationships were more like friendships than romances.

Most of our group outings were on Sundays, when meals were not served at the club. North Beach at that time was popular for Italian or Basque sheep herder family-style dinners, poetry readings at book stores, and for those who could afford it, night clubs, such as the Hungry I and the Purple Onion. Sometimes we ended up at an Italian restaurant with live opera or at the Buena Vista Cafe for Irish coffee. While living in the residence club, I learned to ski at Squaw Valley and Sugar Bowl. On one of those outings, I shall never forget, we ran into a blizzard as we went over Donner Summit when it was my turn to drive.

Most of the young people I met were in their twenties or thirties, and had recently moved to California. They were searching, as I was, for something but exactly what, was not clear. At Langley Porter, we speculated about what some of our patients had taken flight from and what they were seeking. I often asked the same question about my acquaintances and myself. Many of the people I met were suffering from broken marriages or broken relationships; they were wary of establishing relationships of any depth. San Francisco is, and was then, a party town. I hated most parties, found them empty, and, usually, left them feeling a deeper sense of ennui.

Sometimes I was reminded of New York by Turk Murphy's Dixieland Jazz, ethnic restaurants, the San Francisco Opera, and the Art Museums. But I always seemed to find myself contrasting the two cities rather than comparing them. San Francisco was deceptive. It seemed like such a clean and open city in contrast to New York. In Manhattan, I had found jostling with the masses exciting and enjoyed friendly exchanges with vendors on the streets. Exploring ethnic neighborhoods with friends or attending jazz concerts in Greenwich Village and Harlem were usual activities. There, I had felt completely confident I could fend for myself, and considered myself streetwise. But I was neither the sophisticate nor the clever woman I needed to be to handle living in San Francisco. The men I knew in New York were intellectually discerning about art, music, culture, and women, and considered sexual activity a matter of choice and discretion. Here their interest seemed to be focused on big cars or boats, career or financial advancement and "making out," one way or another. My experience in San Francisco was fraught with disappointment, disillusionment, and dangers I had not anticipated. I was wearing a Marilyn Monroe persona of vulnerability while developing the inner core of assurance of a Gloria Steinem, while I traveled in an alien and predatory land.

After the Residence Club, I shared a garden apartment on California Street, sublet a flat in the Haight-Ashbury District, shared a modern apartment with a swimming pool across from Golden Gate Park, and finally, rented a flat of my own on Twin Peaks. Each place had its charm and always a view of San Francisco.

Langley Porter staff members, of all disciplines, extended their hospitality to me and became my friends. I particularly remember a birthday party with a real piñata at Dorothy Gibson's in Sausalito; Thanksgiving in Palo Alto with Lois and Gregory Bateson; Christmas in Yosemite at the Ahwahnee Lodge with Marion Chay and her family. Lida Schneider, supervising P.S.W. in the outpatient clinic and Niki Oswald, supervising P.S.W. of the social work student unit, welcomed me as their sister analysand. They had known Dr. Leslie Farber, my analyst in Washington, D.C., when he was practicing in San Francisco. And I shall never forget Mac, a psychiatric technician, who brought me a stocking one Christmas Eve, when he knew I was absolutely alone and unable to climb up and down three flights of stairs because of a broken ankle.

I suppose it was inevitable that I should find someone with whom I could surround the illusion that I was in love. It didn't take long for a lanky, bona fide Southerner, with soft speech and a quiet manner to appear. He was my age and had never been married. He whisked me away immediately from the party life. I should have known when I met him at the Young Republicans that our values would collide, that our family backgrounds were vastly different, that I did not fit into his country club set, but it took me years to find that out. The simplicity of the activities we enjoyed together—walking among the wild flowers, beach combing, painting, cooking, singing—was misleading. When I was hospitalized with the above mentioned broken ankle, he brought me a hand fashioned flower from a paper towel, and I was completely taken by that simple gesture of affection. I waited for him to establish his business on the peninsula, to grieve the loss of a parent, to travel abroad and on and on. We broke up and reestablished our relationship several times, usually when I was beginning to get interested in someone else.

In one of those disruptions, I enjoyed some of the best times of my San Francisco days with Greg, a friend from the Lafayette Residence Club days. Greg had returned from specialized training in orthodontia in another city and wanted me to see the town with him before he settled into his practice. We went to the best restaurants, nightclubs, the opera, and enjoyed the entertainment we couldn't afford in our Residence Club days. I can still see Greg doing the Charleston. His heart was set on adventure, skiing in the Andes, trekking in the Himalayas, and he did not want to be tied down. A few years later Greg died in an accident in his own plane.

In another of the breaks in my long-term relationship with the Southerner, I became acutely depressed. Staff and patients were experiencing a system crisis at Langley Porter at about the same time. I saw Norman Reider, M.D., a psychoanalyst, who was well known, at Mt. Zion hospital, for brief term psychotherapy. My insights, which were profound for me at the time, included the recognition that I didn't want to be married as much as I had always thought or I would have chosen to marry, but that I was not exactly a spinster; I had no aspirations to become a supervisor, which was the only way one could advance as a psychiatric social worker; what I really wanted was to live more fully as a person.

Living more fully the next few years, I found and furnished my own apartment overlooking the Golden Gate and the green hills of Marin, bought my own piano, and took piano lessons, water color lessons and Chinese brush painting lessons, enjoyed modern dance and began to travel. I made my own curtains, crafted a frame for a mirror of sea-washed glass I found on the beach, hung a branch of manzanita from the Sierra foothills on my wood paneled wall, sank into my solitude, and became domestic.

At a candlelight and wine dinner I had carefully prepared, my long-term friend recognized my affections were deep and informed me, "Merle, you are a normal woman who needs to be married and have a family. They tell me I need psychoanalysis." To be sure I got the message, a short while later, he left a party I was hosting, with an attractive woman who had just arrived in town. On our next date, the only one I had ever initiated, I let him know how deeply hurt and angered I was. We said all the unpleasant things people say in terminating a relationship. I burned, I smoldered, I stung deeply, but I knew we had to part, that he had appraised me accurately. By then I had faced my existential solitude and knew I did not want to spend my life alone.

The glamour of San Francisco was beginning to fade for me at about the same time my professional interests were shifting in a new direction. I was becoming increasingly attracted to what was going on in the larger community, out-

side the confines of Langley Porter. My interest in community organization and social action from graduate school days
surfaced again.

I became the chairperson of the Mental Health Social Action
Committee of the Golden Gate Chapter of NASW. Mental
health legislation was our challenge. This was before NASW had
a legislative advocate in Sacramento. We developed bills to be
introduced in the legislature and tracked them through every
step of the legislative process. We flooded key legislators with letters and telephone calls from NASW members.

I remember a champagne brunch our committee held at
my apartment for one of our targeted legislators. We captured
his attention for the entire afternoon with our stories about the
need for community mental health programs and funding.

After the Short Doyle Community Mental Health Services
Act was passed by the California Legislature in 1957, the State
Department of Mental Hygiene established a ten-year plan for
developing comprehensive community mental health programs
as a preferred alternative to long-term hospitalization in state
hospitals. Attention was given to the possibilities of rehabilitation and prevention of chronicity as well as to making early
treatment available to the total population. The idea was to keep
patients in their home communitites. California had launched
this plan before the Kennedy administration in 1962 unveiled
its bold new program to combat mental illness through early
and complete treatment at community mental health centers,
which was continued by the Johnson administration.

The Center for Training in Community Psychiatry, headed by Portia Bell Hume, M.D., was established in Berkeley in
1961 by the California Department of Mental Hygiene.
Langley Porter encouraged staff and trainees to take courses at
the center as part of their in-service training. Some of my colleagues were already taking jobs in San Mateo County, and in
Berkeley, in new programs, which were becoming recognized
as national models of community mental health programs.

I took the courses the center offered in mental health edu-

cation and mental health consultation, administration, and program evaluation. The practicums for these courses were carefully selected and supervised community projects, which challenged me to integrate all of my training and experience. One
of my projects was to offer mental health consultation to a child
study group of the University Dames, a club of student wives
from the University of California. Use of my total experience in
working with children and families, psychotherapy, group
dynamics, and child development was required to respond
appropriately and effectively on the spot in crisis situations.

My second project at the center was to organize a community in San Mateo County to prepare a halfway house for
patients to be discharged from state mental hospitals. As so
often happens, the novelty of the idea and the enthusiasm of
the community group I was working with, carried the halfway
house into a successful operation. This project was a part of
the California Department of Mental Hygiene Ten-Year Plan
to prepare communities for the return of patients from state
mental hospitals. After Governor Reagan's decision to close
state mental hospitals abruptly went into effect, fierce opposition to a halfway house in any community could be expected.
Local communities were not prepared to accommodate the
onslaught of discharged patients.

Word of my interest in the larger community soon got
around. Isabel Weissman, a colleague and friend from Langley
Porter, was working as a psychiatric social work supervisor for
the Consultation and Education Service in the new City of
Berkeley mental health program. Her enthusiasm was conta-
gious. She urged me to apply for the other psychiatric social
work supervisor position in the new program in the outpatient
psychiatric clinic. I reluctantly agreed because I really did not
want a supervisory job and returned the written application,
but failed to follow through to appear for the scheduled civil
service oral examination.

The City of Berkeley personnel officer called me to
inquire why I had not appeared for the examination. My non-

chalant response that the salary differential was simply insuf-
ficient to interest me in making a move, soon brought a
response. Within days, my interest was piqued by a better
salary offer and a special invitation to meet the Public Health
Director, Alvin Leonard, M.D., the director of Mental Health
Service, Carl Wells, M.D., and the director of the Berkeley-
Herrick Hospital Outpatient Psychiatric Clinic, Eric Plaut,
M.D. Their minds were made up; they wanted me for the job.

I was not interested in sacrificing the freedom I had found
to enjoy a fuller life for additional responsibility. At the same
time, I felt I had reached the saturation point of what I could
expect to learn as a clinician working on the inpatient service
at Langley Porter. Supervisory and administrative positions
offered the only opportunity for advancement in salary for
psychiatric social workers. My interest in developing my clinical skills was my top priority. But I was not sure where that
interest might lead me.

Chapter 11:

TRIAL BY FIRE

City of Berkeley Mental Health
Berkeley, California 1962-1979

I left Langley Porter in 1962 to work in the new community mental health program across the bay from San Francisco in Berkeley. As I approached my forties, I had no way of knowing what major changes the next decade would bring in my life or what the 60s would bring us all. I was moving into an exciting and chaotic period personally, and into the socio-political upheaval of the times. Berkeley was to become my home but I would never have believed it then.

The Berkeley mental health program was part of the cutting edge of community mental health in California. After five years of working with hospitalized psychiatric patients, I found the preventive focus of this new program very attractive. There was no way I could have known then how controversial community mental health would become in California, a decade later.

When I kept my appointment for the interview in Berkeley with the director of public health, the mental health service chief and the director of the Herrick Hospital–City of Berkeley Outpatient Psychiatric Clinic, they pressed me to take the job as the supervising psychiatric social worker in the Outpatient Psychiatric Clinic. My experience at Langley Porter combined with public welfare, child welfare, and child guidance experience, under state and local, public and private auspices, was highly desirable for community mental health leadership. Moreover, I had skills in administration and consultation, and I was enrolled at the Center for Training in Community Psychiatry. There was a shortage of trained clinical personnel at that time; many of those who had clinical experience were neither interested in nor informed about community mental health.

I knew that administrative responsibility was demanding, leaving little time or space for oneself. I was reluctant to leave San Francisco and to give up the freedom I had found to enjoy other aspects of life. But I bargained for what I wanted most— the opportunity to develop my clinical skills.

They assured me that, in addition to my supervisory responsibilities, I would have a small caseload with clinical supervision and psychiatric consultation. The crowning attraction for me was the collegial atmosphere, the assurance of professional autonomy, and the promise of clinical experience with adults, families, and children. Upon learning I would not be required to live in Berkeley, that the commute against traffic would be easy, I could not resist being in on the ground floor of this exciting new program.

The Berkeley program was one of three community mental health programs in California. The Department of Health and Welfare in San Mateo County, on the peninsula, below San Francisco, had established mental health services a year after the Community Mental Health Service Act was passed by the California Legislature in 1957. There was one new program in southern California, in Pasadena. The Berkeley Health

Department offered an ideal setting for the development of a program in the San Francisco Bay Area. The director of the Health Department was on the faculty at the University of California School of Public Health. There were strong linkages with the Berkeley Unified School District, police department, private agencies, and hospitals.

The Berkeley Health Department established mental health services in 1961 with the appointment of a program chief and a mental health advisory board. The program's initial focus was on prevention. The mental health education and mental health consultation service was already in operation with a staff of psychiatrists, psychiatric social workers, a mental health educator, and a mental health nurse.

In 1962, the program was augmented by direct clinical services. The Herrick-Berkeley Outpatient Psychiatric Clinic located at Herrick Hospital was jointly administered by the Health Department and Herrick Hospital. That hospital had a well-known inpatient psychiatric service, one of the oldest in California; a training program for psychiatric residents; and a psychiatric emergency service. Combining public and private resources was an important part of community mental health planning.

Eric Plaut, M.D., director of the Herrick-Berkeley Outpatient Clinic, was appointed by the City of Berkeley and by Herrick Hospital and he was also on the faculty of the University of California Medical School. Well-grounded psychodynamically and psychoanalytically, he brought ambition, and strong leadership in setting up the clinic to include the psychiatric outpatient residency training as well as service to the community. He translated his experience with brief term psychotherapy at Kaiser Permanente and the Cowell Psychiatric Clinic at the University of California into a vision of no waiting list for treatment. The explanation was simple: each staff member was expected to see a certain number of new patients each week with no exceptions and was provided supervision, consultation, and clinical conferences. For their own professional development, staff and trainees were expected to have some longer-term treatment cases.

As the supervising psychiatric social worker, I maintained my professional autonomy, but I think there is little question that I also served as a handmaiden to psychiatry, a role often attributed to social workers in psychiatric clinics at that time. Dr. Plaut worked half time at the clinic; I was in charge in his absence. I assisted him with administration, recruitment and selection of staff and trainees, program development and evaluation, coordination of treatment and training activities. I also coordinated fieldwork for social work students from the University of California School of Social Welfare, and provided consultation to interdisciplinary staff and trainees.

By the time I had taken the easy commute against traffic for a year, Berkeley began to look more attractive as a place to live. I was pleased to find a modern apartment out of the San Francisco fog in a new building near the University. The deer still grazed on the hillside under my deck; my privacy there was blissful. There was a place for my piano, a wall for my paintings, a swimming pool, a sun deck, and a convenient kitchen for entertaining. I swam every day, continued my piano lessons, enjoyed my Chinese brush painting, joined a modern dance group, and made new friends in Berkeley.

The Herrick-Berkeley Adult Outpatient Clinic grew and flourished. The training program expanded until at one time we had forty-five trainees, including psychiatric residents, social work students, psychology interns, and clinical pastoral counselor trainees. The outpatient treatment time grew to more than 1000 hours per month serving predominantly young people of the 60s.

There was lots of supervision, consultation, teamwork, and innovation. The staff of the clinic and the staff of the mental health consultation and education services exchanged duties and attendance at conferences so that all staff members had experience in both psychotherapy and indirect services in the community. We established a childrens' service and brought in consultants for training in group therapy and family therapy. The clinic's training program was a popular one for trainees of different disciplines and for staff as well. Individuals from different professional disciplines worked well together. Clinical conferences were stimulating. Focus on brief term therapy fit with prevalent theories of that era—ego-oriented psychotherapy (Heinz Hartman, M.D.) and crisis intervention (Eric Lindeman, M.D., Mary Sarvis, M.D., and Lydia Rappaport, P.S.W.). The atmosphere was exciting. Morale was high. Working in the Clinic was a heady trip.

The 60s was a stressful time for students. Many of them took time out from college for moratoria or dropped out in a crisis or, in all good conscience, sought psychiatric certification to evade the draft. The majority of the persons seen at the Adult Outpatient Clinic were between the ages of eighteen and twenty-four, tapering off into the thirties. Most of them had recently been enrolled as undergraduate or graduate students at the University of California and other colleges in the area.

Berkeley reflected and fermented the social change and political turmoil of the 60s. The continuous threat of the atom bomb and the Cuban missile crisis of 1962; the civil rights movement and the Mississippi freedom summer of 1964, which was led by the Student Non-violent Coordinating Committee, and drew a large contingent of University of California and Bay Area students to the south; the student sit-ins and arrests in the free speech movement in the fall of 1964; Vietnam War protests; the People's Park incidents with the National Guard and tear gas on the streets of Berkeley in 1969; the passive protests of the flower children; the sexual freedom movement and the growing drug culture were a part of that environment.

Some of the experiences I recall that took me into the inner life of the young people the clinic served included: my terror of the atom bomb during the Cuban missile crisis that made me appreciate the ever constant fear that hung over students' heads in the cold war; seeing the intense involvement of some of my students, colleagues and friends, including university faculty, in the free speech movement; working with young persons who lost brothers, lovers, or friends in Vietnam; the chilling fear of seeing the National Guard on the streets of Berkeley in one of the People's Park incidents; working in the emergency room at Herrick Hospital on "Bloody Thursday" as the injured and maimed were brought off the streets; finding my young relative, Allen, safe in his apartment across Telegraph Avenue from where James Rector was shot; hearing the stories of staff, trainees, and patients who were rounded up and taken to jail in paddy wagons by the "Blue Meanies," from the Alameda County Sheriff's Department; marching in the Vietnam War protests.

The case histories of those young people, many of whom were labeled by the public as hippies, dropouts, pot heads, or draft dodgers, have long since been destroyed, as the law permits, after six years. But I picture them, individually and collectively, in my mind's eye, as I have had occasion to do many times as a clinician.

I think of Byran as a prototypical example. At eighteen, he was an exceptionally bright and personable young man, who dropped out of college before the end of the first semester against the entreaty of his father, his professors, and the dean. He was referred by his friends, who saw therapy as a safe thing to do if one was "hung-up." He had lots of labels for his hang-up, all the way from manic-depressive to schizophrenic, but mainly, he felt confused. His father, a World War II veteran, saw him as a draft dodger, his girlfriend was pushing him for a sexual relationship, the Welfare Department, to which he had applied for Aid To The Disabled, was pressing him to get a statement of psychiatric disability, which he hoped he could also use for exemption from the draft board. There was only one thing he was sure of. He wanted to be his "own agent." He didn't want a therapist telling him what to do.

I saw Bryan the day after he telephoned the clinic vaguely

hinting at suicidal thoughts, and twice a week for the next month, at the end of which time, he was a planning to take a full-time job and return to college.

The content and dynamics of what transpired between Bryan and me in those eight sessions are too complex to report here, but it was clear Bryan transferred onto me, as his therapist, feelings about paternal authority and fears he would lose me as he had lost his mother, at an early age.

The picture of his identity crisis, with all its unresolved conflicts, emerged in bold relief, and strongly suggested that his self-imposed moratorium was necessary before he could move ahead.

Bryan, as many of his cohorts, had to deal with his conflict about seeking psychiatric disability for an exemption from the draft.

◉   ◉   ◉   ◉   ◉

The 60s brought many changes in my personal life as I grew and matured and made new friends in Berkeley. I never had felt quite so sure of myself or so confident that each day would bring its own rewards. I was enjoying life, as I promised myself I would when I was in San Francisco. My new friends in Berkeley included some of those safety net friends with young families who had small children. I helped to prepare their nurseries and rocked their infants with a painful awareness of not having babies of my own. My biological clock was ticking.

Recognition of my own mortality hit me as the losses and eye openers of mid-life began to strike in rapid succession. My brother and his wife separated after thirteen years of marriage. I found there was absolutely nothing I could do to help either of them with the turmoil they were in. My friend, Marion McCraney and her husband, Bruce, were killed in an automobile accident shortly after I last saw them during a visit to Arlington. Greg, who had been a good friend since I arrived in

San Francisco, was killed in an accident in his airplane. My father died after an extended illness with an inoperable brain tumor. I watched television reports of John F. Kennedy's assassination in the hospital at Leesburg, Virginia, after spending the night with my family in a deathwatch at my father's bedside. The two events were forever linked.

My parents had visited me shortly before my father's illness in 1963 and helped me look at houses I might consider buying in Berkeley. They wanted me to have a home, married or not, "A nice little starter house."

In 1964, I looked at a house in the Berkeley Hills and bought it that afternoon. David Malcom, the realtor, had never sold a house before and I had never bought one. We made a deal and he sent me roses.

I had looked at a lot of houses by then; this one stole my heart. A bungalow built in the 20s had been converted into a library by a Chinese professor, who left bookshelves in every room. He had it redecorated by a designer before he put it on the market. The house overlooked San Francisco Bay, the Golden Gate Bridge, and the Oakland Bay Bridge, and had a garden filled with roses and honeysuckle. Enormous eucalyptus and redwood trees sheltered it for privacy. A grand piano in the empty family room, and an architect's drafting table in the den looked lost. The house, freshly painted and carefully arranged for showing, was much smaller than it appeared, but quite large enough for my things. There was no way to know then that my home would become a family home.

A few years later, Bob Davis and I were married in a simple wedding ceremony in the only chapel in the Berkeley hills, the Lutheran Church of The Cross. June 11, 1967 was a sunny, clear, beautiful day. I wore a white linen dress and white lace coat and carried a bouquet of blue delphiniums. We vowed "to try to make a good marriage," a vow we have repeated many times since. We laughed on the way to the church as I brushed the flour out of my hair and off my hands from making rolls for the reception. Our wedding was small; our champagne reception in our new home was joyously gaudy with live music.

Soon afterward, and for a long time since, I realized that my life with Bob was more satisfying than any romantic illusion I had held before. Besides that, he cooked our breakfast. He was also from the country—rural Maine. Our professional interests were complementary; he had a master's degree in public health from the University of California, Berkeley. His children from a previous marriage—Chuck, a thirteen year-old-boy and Jennifer, a five-year-old girl—were with us for most weekends, holidays, and vacations.

I felt pleased to have this much family life after waiting so long. While I knew I would find it difficult not to become overly attached to a little girl, who lived in the area with her mother, I was not sure how it would be to become the step-mother of an adolescent boy. Soon I found out; he came to live with us to finish high school in the 60s.

Fortunately, the work I had done in family therapy had taught me the impossibility of blending families. I did not try. My husband felt it was in the best interest of the children, to support their view of their original home as their primary home. We welcomed them and enjoyed having them visit us but we did not encourage them to think of our home as their second home. I found it difficult to accept this as I wanted them to have a place in our home. But I knew from my work, that for children, their family of origin always has the central place in their view of family and I tried to respect that. I think I was viewed more like an aunt or an extended family member than as a stepmother or parent, at least initially.

In our marriage, I found, for the first time, that I could be myself in a relationship with a man. Bob claimed that it was that very quality of authenticity that attracted him. We worked hard to communicate with one another directly our affectionate feelings and our disagreements. To find I could be angry with someone and survive it, and that I could tolerate the anger of another person in a relationship, was a new experience for me. I had never dreamed of the intimacy that we found and the joy it brought as we built a relationship that sustained us through difficult times ahead.

Bob was working in Berkeley's housing program and teaching at Chabot College in Hayward, at the same time. We respected and supported one another's career paths and endeavors. We were different people and we had different interests, different opinions, and different friends. But we had much in common. We both liked a simple life and enjoyed outdoor activities, music, reading, and our home. We usually took Bob's children with us on our vacations. In Virginia, we visited with my family on the farm, and in Maine we visited with Bob's parents at their Lakeview Inn on Sebago Lake. Those were some of the happiest times in our early marriage.

In the late 60s, the socio-political changes of the era coincided with efforts of the City of Berkeley and Herrick Hospital to seek Federal funding for a community mental health center. As plans moved forward, a complete change took place in the top administration of Berkeley Mental Health. When Carl Wells, M.D., mental health chief retired for health reasons in 1968, Eric Plaut, M.D., was appointed acting mental health chief until he resigned in 1969. Alvin Leonard, M.D., Director of the Berkeley Health Department, resigned in 1969 to take a teaching position in Colorado.

Neal Blumenfeld, M.D., who headed the psychiatric residency training in the clinic and was a popular teacher for all disciplines, was offered the position as director of the clinic. He accepted it, but refused to continue in that position after six months.

Before Dr. Plaut left Berkeley Mental Health he appealed to me to take the position as acting head of the clinic. I don't think I fully understood the implications of his entreaty when he told me, "Merle, I don't know whether you will consider this a compliment or an insult, but I think you are the only staff person who can hold the clinic together." The staff was already beginning to feel intense pressure from various self-styled activist groups. No explanation of our brief term thera-

py focus was credible to these groups who opposed psychoanalysis and were convinced the clinic's approach was exclusively psychoanalytic. One of our psychiatric consultants
raised the question in a staff meeting concerning the wisdom
of remaining on the staff. He said "You have been here almost
a decade and developed a program you are proud of. Things
change; maybe it is time to move on." Not one of the rest of
us left the clinic at that time.

◉   ◉   ◉   ◉   ◉

I found myself in the position of temporary acting director of the clinic for the next two years, 1969-1971, without
commensurate pay or Civil Service classification. For the following two years, 1971-73, I served in the same capacity as
special assistant mental health program coordinator (provisional) with a five percent pay increase.

In 1970, Herrick Hospital, with the participation of the
City of Berkeley's Health Department, set up a community
mental health center believing federal funding would become
available. A new director and associate director, both well
known psychoanalysts from the East Coast were brought in,
and new programs were set up to meet the federal require-
ments for a community mental health center; a methadone
treatment program; a day treatment center; a crisis intervention service, and expanded family, youth, and children's services. We already had an inpatient service and an outpatient
clinic.

From the beginning of my effort to tell the story of my life
and work as a social worker, I have known the 70s would be
the most difficult decade for me to recount, not only because
of the complexity of that era but also because they were the
most demanding and intense years of my career and my life.

I had a strong conviction that the expanded services
required of a community mental health center did not require
sacrificing the quality of professional clinical services the clin-

ic staff had worked so hard to develop. I had an equally strong belief that a wider segment of the community needed to be served. Often, I felt caught between my loyalty to my professional colleagues in the clinic and my responsibility for the clinic's program to the top administration of the community mental health center.

Shirley Cooper, LCSW, a contemporary and role model I have admired since I arrived in the Bay area, was chief social worker at Mt. Zion Hospital in San Francisco. She captured the dilemma I experienced in her paper in a special issue of the *Clinical Social Worker Journal* in 1977:

"There are very real tensions between professional behavior and values and those which profess to maximize efficiency in organizations. Suffice it to say that bureaucracies value uniformity, rules of operation with minimal exception, control, accountability, coordination, and role authority. Professionals value diversity, individualized understanding, autonomy, personal authority, and responsibility."

Despite extensive efforts of the administration and staff, and widely expanded services, the federal funding for the community mental health center never came to fruition. As best that I can recall, the publicly stated reason had to do with the lack of participation from the community in the planning process. Two clear recollections stand out: the adult outpatient clinic staff's input concerning involvement of the community was neither sought nor invited by Herrick Hospital or the City of Berkeley, and in disorderly meetings swarms of activist groups representing different factions of the community protested their lack of participation. I later understood that private psychiatrists who had staff privileges at Herrick Hospital also actively opposed the community mental health center.

A change in national policy with the advent of the Nixon administration meant that funding for community mental health centers would now be allocated through the community block grants. Local politics also changed. A battle for control ensued between the state and local governments. The dream of a community mental health center went down the drain in a struggle on the local level over whether the City of Berkeley or Herrick Hospital would be the recipient and have control of the funding from Alameda County.

In 1972, the efforts of the previous decade to combine public and private community resources for mental health in Berkeley, broke down completely. The city mental health services were separated, administratively and physically, from Herrick Hospital. My colleague, Isabel Weissman, supervising P.S.W., became the acting director of Berkeley Mental Health Services until 1974, when she retired, after she was failed on the oral civil service examination for the job she had already done for two years on a temporary basis. This same thing happened in at least one, and possibly, other city departments at about the same. Early retirement was encouraged by the city.

I felt deeply about the humiliation my friend Isabel experienced. Her leadership had been important in the development of Berkeley's mental health services. We had been through a lot together, from appearing at City Council meetings on behalf of the program, to joining the public employees union (SEIU) and striking alongside the garbage workers for better wages for psychiatric social workers. I shall never forget the day David Aaroner, representative for SEIU 535, successfully negotiated for the destruction of the written reprimand that the city administration had ordered to go into our personnel files because we had stood up for professional standards of practice.

I entered the last phase of my civil service with the City of Berkeley in 1973 before Isabel's departure. The stress of the previous years caught up with me. When I was faced with ovarian cancer, a life threatening condition that necessitated a total hysterectomy, I requested a demotion from the provisional clinic coordinator position. From that time until I retired in 1979, I retained my permanent supervising psychiatric social worker classification. Recovering from surgery that summer, I listened to the Watergate hearings, which reflected the disillusionment of the country. I thought that I had never felt as bereft as I contemplated the lessons the youth of the 60s had tried to teach us.

My fiftieth birthday was in the midst of a season of loss. A close friend died of cancer, the first of several losses of contemporaries, which is one of the true warnings of midlife. Our son left home and college in an emotional farewell scene giving us a foretaste of the empty nest. And our daughter, at the age of eleven, looked up at the stars one night as we sat outside and said, "I wish I never had to grow up," undoubtedly sensing the pain of her elders.

What was I to do? Facing my mortality squarely, the answer was clear. "Do the best you can for yourself and your clients in the situation you are in." Some of my colleagues were moving into private practice after the licensing of clinical social workers went into effect in California in 1969, but I did not feel I could make a change at that time. We had children to educate. I was caught in the Civil Service bind.

My husband, who also worked for the City of Berkeley, faced organizational changes in his department similar to those that I faced. Sharing these changes over dinner offered mutual support to one another, but it increased our anxiety. Our aim was to stick it out until we could take early retirement.

In 1975, we bought a small piece of land in the Sierra foothills. We could hear the coyotes and the night sounds of crickets and frogs in our pond. With our own hands, Bob and I built our rustic cabin as a retreat. Our place in the country helped us preserve our sanity and, in time, helped us to move out of the City of Berkeley Civil Service. On our way back to Berkeley, one weekend in 1978, we made a decision that our survival was more important than toughing it out. Bob resigned the next day.

I tried in those last years of the 70s to maintain a low profile in the administrative hierarchy, to focus on the work that needed to be done, to learn as much as I could clinically in the space that had opened up for me to see more patients. I worked on a crisis intervention team in the crisis center, and on an immediate treatment team of interdisciplinary staff, trainees, and volunteers in the clinic. I supervised graduate social work students from the University of California School of Social Welfare and San Francisco State University, and consulted with professional and nonprofessional volunteers in the clinic.

After a Berkeley Mental Health Advisory Board task force identified the aging as an underserved population, program development accelerated and in 1975, at the insistence of the Gray Panthers, a public commitment was made that ten percent of the mental health budget and program would be devoted to mental health services for the senior population. I was asked to head up a sub-clinic for mental health services for the aging as a part of the outpatient clinic.

Trainees, who were specializing in working with the aging, were selected, volunteers with special interests or skills were recruited, and all staff and trainees were expected to participate in the clinic for the aging. In-service training for staff, trainees, and out-reach workers was emphasized. Regular case conferences and community agency network conferences identified the need for protective services for the frail elderly. Models were developed for in-home assessment and for ongoing supportive services to the isolated, homebound aged. Psychotherapy as well as medication was offered in the clinic. Models for group therapy for persons over 60 were developed.

As a result of the sensitization of the clinic staff to the special needs and issues in working with the aging, and increased outreach activity, the percentage of older persons seen in the clinic increased markedly. Volunteers and professionals from the community gave generously of their time. Once more, I found my part in the development of a new program exciting. Working in tandem with the Gray Panthers, we begin to see new programs for seniors, including plans for three new senior centers, develop in Berkeley.

In the late 70s, another change in local Berkeley politics resulted in the elimination of six clinical positions from the adult outpatient clinic staff. These cuts included nearly all of my clinical colleagues I had worked with since the beginning of the program. When the city asked a volunteer to head the sub-clinic on aging in 1979, I made a decision to take early retirement because, I felt I could no longer offer effective leadership in developing mental health services for the aging in the Berkeley community by remaining in the program.

The day after I retired, I drove by the clinic on my way to the farmer's market for produce. I could now shop for vegetables like other homemakers. I had not expected the relief and pleasure that I felt with the closing of this chapter of my life. I had no tears, no lump in the throat. There was no gold watch, no official recognition of my retirement, but at a surprise farewell party informally planned by friends, colleagues, and students, I had felt both sadness and joy. I very much appreciated their tribute. They presented me with a plaque from the California General Assembly recognizing my years of public service, a hand-made ceramic cup with a red heart handle, a tin box of jellybeans, along with a prankster's silly clown's mask with a red nose to keep me cheerful. Pictures of that party capture my feeling of lightness of being, of feeling as good about myself as I had on my wedding day. I was surrounded by the support of those colleagues and friends who meant the most to me. That confidence carried me into the future on a cloud. Was this the beginning of letting go?

I had spent almost two decades during the prime time of my adult life, in the Berkeley Mental Health Services. My attachment was deep. Several months later, when I was attending psychiatric rounds at Herrick Hospital, now Alta Bates Hospital, meetings that I still attend, I realized I had an institutional transference to the place.

It was at Herrick Hospital that I walked the corridors in blind grief over the death of my father. There, my boss, Eric Plaut, M.D., was shocked at receiving an invitation to my wedding. It was while I was there I resolved my conflict about marriage and career, and established my marriage, home and family in the Berkeley hills. At the same time, I realized the linear peak of my career ladder. At Herrick, I made and lost most of my close friends, who were colleagues, as they went in different directions upon leaving the clinic and, unfortunately, seemed to feel as split off from one another as they felt from Berkeley Mental Health Services. It was there the challenges, crises, and changes in mid-life, and the socio-political changes over which I had no control contributed to serious health problems and early retirement at the age of 56, with reduced retirement benefits, and a devastating sense of loss, but not failure.

In the years that followed my leaving the clinic, I was fortunate to have the opportunity to integrate the trauma of the 60s and the optimism and promise that era foretold. As I think of the youth who were the predominant clientele of the Herrick-Berkeley outpatient psychiatric clinic, I think of their advocacy for peace and a more open society and for the gains we are making in that direction.

And, as for my own professional and personal development, I look upon the 70s as an enriching experience in multi-cultural and multiracial relationships. I learned a new dimension of community organization, not only from Saul Alinsky and my observation of the Berkeley scene, but also from organizing mental health services for the aging.

I found multi-disciplinary training, particularly the training of social workers, one of the most satisfying experiences of my career. I was more committed to the benefits of psychotherapy than ever. And for all the controversy about community mental health, I would support any movement in the future that focused on prevention and intervention.

A Collage I made in art class in 1990—includes pictures of family seals, parents, the Shenandoah Valley of Virginia, Fauquier County (The County Courthouse, Wesley Chapel, Hume School), San Francisco and the Sierra Nevada foothills which remind me of the Blue Ridge Mountain foothills

Bob

Retirement party given by friends when I left Berkeley Mental Health, 1979.

Merle at Stonehenge

V. THE RETURN

Integration and Reflection

1979-1997

Merle and her friend Ruth Gubler Kluge at
Mary Washington College, 1944 and 50 years later
when they returned for their class reunion

Chapter 12:

RETURNING HOME-
COMPLETING THE CIRCLE

Berkeley, California

We shall not cease from exploration
And the end of all our exploring
Will be to arrive where we started
And know the place for the first time.....

A condition of complete simplicity
(Costing not less than everything)
And all shall be well
All manner of thing shall be well.......

—*Little Gidding* by T.S. Eliot

Soon after I retired from the City of Berkeley mental health service in 1979, I established my private practice in clinical social work in Berkeley and Albany, an adjoining city.

While I had mixed feelings about adding another chapter to my professional life, Bob knew better than I that I was not finished, that I needed a retreat to collect my thoughts. When the opportunity presented itself to lease an office in a quiet neighborhood near our home, he urged me to take it. And I found to quote Virginia Wolf, "A room of one's own" at work was as important as a personal space at home.

Private practice was a good choice, giving me the opportunity for replenishment and integration. I had time to reflect on my previous experience as new case situations required, time to study, to round out my clinical skills, and eventually time to let go. It was like coming home to my profession, to my own identity as a clinical social worker. At the same time it was like coming home to my community and home in Berkeley, and to myself.

I made an intentional choice to balance my time for my personal life and my practice. The limits I set for myself were clear. The flow of referrals was steady with few dramatic markers from one year to the next. I usually worked about half-time, which freed me to take more responsibility in community and professional activities.

There was a striking parallel between the integrative processes in my work and in my personal life. I had another chance to develop interests I had not had much time for: homemaking, painting, gardening, travelling, renewing old friendships, making new friends. New challenges, and new demands, the continuing losses of mid-life made my dealing with old conflicts essential. Looking back and re-ordering what really mattered became mandatory. The transitions in the aging process as I moved from my mid-fifties, through my sixties and into my seventies, though not easier than other transitions, provided me with new opportunities for growth and maturation.

My office was located in a small yellow house, remodeled with four offices and two waiting rooms, across the street from a new library and community center. Vines covered the office building's windows for privacy. An enclosed garden was accessible. What a refuge for professional solitude after thirty-five years in a public setting!

I took my time furnishing and decorating my office and setting up my professional library. Two Scandinavian leather chairs and a footstool were my biggest luxury. They were so comfortable for a tired back and neck—worn out from sitting at desks of improper height in chairs that aggravated the discomfort. I brought a desk, some lamps, tables and paintings from home. And real oriental rugs were placed on the floor. For a short while I sat enjoying my books, then my first referrals stirred my excitement about having my own practice. Soon, other therapists in the building wanted to plan an open house to announce our arrival in the community. A child psychiatrist, a Jungian analyst, a psychologist, and two clinical social workers threw a party in the garden. After the open house, I was in business. Referrals from professional colleagues were always my best source of clientele.

Before I had my business cards and announcements printed, I carefully considered what I would focus on, what I would announce as my specialization. For too long, I had put administration and program needs ahead of my interest in clinical work. Now I had the opportunity to choose what I wanted to do. Working with older persons and their families was recognized in the community as a specialization that I had developed in recent years. I enjoyed consultation and knew there was a need for it in developing programs and facilities for elderly persons. Working with children and adolescents, as well as adults in psychotherapy, were also special interests. I enjoyed doing family therapy. But I found that delineating generic interest and specific skills was not much easier than it had ever been.

Helen Harris Perlman said, "Most Social Workers are born in the briar patch of Social Work." For me, the rest of the fable, "Mr. Farmer, please don't throw me in the briar patch," simply means I was most familiar with the stickiest parts. I was reputed to work with difficult cases in the clinic, meaning I usually got the cases that nobody was willing to see and I learned how to work with them. While I continued to work with so-called difficult cases in my private practice, my case-load was a cross-sectional mix, diverse in age, race, ethnic background, socio-economic status, and psychiatric diagnoses. Life-threatening illnesses such as AIDS, heart disease, cancer, and other chronic illnesses and disabilities were sometimes involved. I saw families of all ages, allowing me a review of developmental levels, and I found the greatest challenge in my work with the aged, whether individuals or families.

Soon after I opened my office, Mr. and Mrs. A, a couple, in their 60s, who were referred by the police, sought family therapy after their adult son, Roger, who lived in their home, was charged with elder abuse. Roger refused to attend the dual diagnosis day treatment program to which he had been referred by the court. His parents hoped that I could engage him. Multiple addictions, serious illness, a long history of dysfunction were a part of the family picture. Violence characterized the family's way of life. After his siblings and the extended family were included in the family therapy sessions, at Roger's insistence, he returned to his treatment program and found a place to live out of the parental home. I felt I learned more than I offered in this case, but the family, Roger, the day treatment center staff, and the police were pleased with the result.

I knew that elder abuse was becoming an increasingly recognized problem. Learning about child abuse was not a new experience, but witnessing it, and being required by law to report it was. I was jarred emotionally when a young mother who had sought therapy for help in dealing with her uncontrollable, abusive behavior toward her four-year-old child, demonstrated that behavior toward the child in my office. She knew I was required to report it. After that, I had to report the abuse of a child, who had been locked in solitary confinement in her room for a week with only bread and water for nourishment. I found the unconcerned bravado of the parents so anxiety provoking that I ended up at the hospital emergency room thinking I was having a heart attack.

Some of my cases included: a mother whose child had been diagnosed with leukemia, a young woman who was trying to decide whether to continue with her plans for marriage after receiving treatment for breast cancer, a seventy-two-year-old man who was depressed following a stroke. So much for the long-term intensive psychotherapy I had been led to believe took place in private practice. My sights turned toward more active participation in the professional community and in the community at large, which became a part of the organic process of my practice.

From 1979-1984, I served as the community representative on the Committee for the Protection of Human Subjects at the University of California, Berkeley. Protocols for all research involving humans, directly or indirectly, were reviewed and approved or disapproved. Serving on this committee was a new experience, a reversal of roles for me to represent the community with academia. Reading the protocols took a lot of time but activated my brain cells and stretched my mind.

I served on the coordinating committee for twenty-four senior activity centers for BACS-Bay Area Community Services. Most of the activity centers had been established by the East Bay Council of Churches twenty years before for seniors in their sixties. They were confronted with making the necessary changes to serve clients who were now in their eighties and nineties. Some of the centers were converted to day care centers for persons suffering from Alzheimer's disease or Alzheimer's-like syndromes.

After serving on the board of the East Bay Clinic for Psychotherapy, a non-profit clinic in Oakland, I was invited to join their staff to help set up a mental health program for the aging. From 1981-1985, I worked there half-time. The clinic was organized and established by two clinical social workers who had been among the social work students at the Herrick-Berkeley outpatient clinic and by two psychiatrists. It offered services no longer available in public programs, such as long-term treatment for low income people, and people on Medi-Cal and Medicare and long-term, low fee treatment for children in foster care and for their foster families.

The East Bay Clinic's services for older persons soon became recognized in the community. We offered consultation to hospitals, senior residential facilities, and community agencies, developed a training program for interdisciplinary interns specializing in clinical work with the aging. In addition to offering clinical services for older persons and their families, we continued to develop a model for psychotherapy groups for women over 60 and for family caretaker groups. I learned from my social work intern, who already had her graduate degree with a specialization in aging and from a clinical social worker colleague, who was our group therapy consultant. And we all learned together. This helped me in phasing back into spending more time in my clinical work with older patients in my private practice.

My interest in working with older persons became my focus. By this time I had seen a lot of older people who were in their 60s, 70s, 80s, even 90s, in psychotherapy. Contrary to the popular view then that older people were unwilling to use mental health services and resistant to therapy, I found that once a working relationship was established, they not only used psychotherapy well, but also valued it. Those who had had therapy in earlier years used it even better.

Freud believed psychoanalysis was contraindicated for persons over fifty. Erickson saw the fruition of the developmental process in the resolution of the conflict between personal integrity and despair by the older adult. Jung saw the second half of life, i.e., after fifty years of age, as offering the opportunity for the old as well as the young to grow psychologically toward the fulfillment of their psychic potential.

My experience in developing mental health services for the

aging led me to believe that older persons had strikingly similar concerns, whether they were diagnosed as having serious psychiatric conditions or whether they were from the general population experiencing stress due to the aging process.

Stresses and crises are difficult to separate. Developmental crises and situational crises are not easy to differentiate, especially when we know so little about the developmental phases of the last fifty years—the "young old," the "older old," even the "oldest old." If you think of it, these later years cover a developmental span at least as wide as the first fifty. Therapy can facilitate the developmental process and prevent or shake loose impasses, which sometimes result in serious psychological problems. Crisis intervention theory based on timely intervention, strength of the ego, and removing impediments to developmental progress fits nicely with the inner resourcefulness of a lifetime of older persons. It takes only a slight turn of the imagination to see some of the defenses professionals examine with a finely-tuned ear as coping mechanisms.

In the older population, a crisis frequently precipitates the request for therapy—illness, loss of a loved one, changes in life style, transitions, such as, a move from home to institution, change in geographic location. The case of Mrs. Z. informs us of some of the crises and vulnerability to stress even the sturdiest of us might encounter in growing older and of the capacity of older persons to use ongoing therapy. Mrs. Z, age seventy-two, sought therapy complaining of an impending sense of doom, which she attributed to her fear of a stroke or a heart attack that would leave her husband unprotected. She was under a doctor's care for three chronic conditions: hypertension, diabetes, and arthritis. Her husband was diagnosed with Alzheimer's disease and was becoming a management problem. Both his neurologist and her children urged her to place him in a convalescent home. But she was ambivalent and uneasy that the cost of custodial care would exhaust their financial resources. Physical abuse was threatening. She said she understood her husband was not himself, and "he was always such a good man," but sometimes he seemed to sense her anger and resentment and react to it. She had to laugh at herself for toppling him with her walker when he came at her.

Mrs. Z. became acutely depressed when she placed her husband in a convalescent home. Her preoccupation with her own death became more sharply focused. She was surprised when I told her I thought her depression was understandable. In the next hour, she told me her daughter had said, "Mother, when you think of all the losses you have had in the last few years, why wouldn't you be depressed?" She said she simply had never thought of herself as being depressed, but it was not as if she were a stranger to loss. Facing the loss of her husband was different though. In one respect, she thought she had already mourned his loss; in other respects, she had to continually deal with her emotional responses to the physical body that was only the shell of his former self.

Mrs. Z. continued in individual and group therapy for more than a year. As she found a release of energy from dealing with her anger and resentment, and encountered aspects of herself she had not recognized before, neglected potential abilities became available to her. She began to write poetry. She was in touch with her inclination to turn her attention to her inner thoughts after her lifetime of primarily focusing on others. She had used casework services from Family Service when her children were small, but this was the first time she had focused on herself.

Basic social work principles were as essential at the end of my career in working with older persons as they were at the beginning. Honoring the uniqueness of each individual, and respect for human dignity and diversity, were never more important as I tried to understand the whole person—body, mind and spirit. I found that a therapist's respect for older persons' ability to be self-determining could be crucial in their maintaining that ability.

In a family therapy session with her sons, Mrs. H., an eighty-two-year-old widow, plaintively stated her desire to remain in her own convenient and attractive townhouse. Her sons were insisting that she move to a tri-level residential care facility. The sons said they needed to feel secure about their mother's safety, and, to avoid the possibility that she would call on them for help, in the event she became incapacitated.

I asked Mrs. H. to outline for her sons her plans for her self-maintenance, which I knew, had been well thought out from our work in individual therapy. I encouraged her to tell them about her hopes for social interchange and cultural enrichment in her own community. The sons were touched in hearing her speak of her longing for some of the pleasures she had deprived herself of for so many years while taking care of their father. She wanted to entertain her friends, to go to the symphony, to tend her deck garden with outside help that was available and she could afford. She reminded them that she was prepared to use her extensive experience gained as their father's caretaker in making plans for her own care. They agreed to her plan for the immediate future, and then they and she, renegotiated a plan for her long-term care.

Longer-term psychotherapy with older persons taught me a lot about the resilience and possibilities of growth and change in this population. I think of Mr. D., a distinguished scholar in his eighties, a widower, who sought therapy to deal with his guilt about not having been more outgoing and considerate of his faithful wife of many years. Suffering with depression and serious illness, he complained of his irascible behavior toward his friends, who expected him to reciprocate their hospitality. A few months before his death, he planned and executed a dinner party for his friends to his great satisfaction. He saw this as an accomplishment in overcoming his passivity, a character trait, which he had struggled with all of his life.

I also think of Mrs. F., a woman I saw for five years, after she had spent a year in a rehabilitation center following a stroke at the age of sixty-eight. Her recovery, which was completely supported by her family, friends, and community, was slow, but she found a new life as an artist, maintained herself independently, and fell in love in her seventies.

Family therapy was one of the integrative challenges for me. The families who found their way to my office provided me the opportunity to pull together all the experience and training I had acquired through the years. Pursuing my interest in working with older persons and their families, I saw close at hand the intergenerational conflicts as well as stresses of the modern family.

For instance, I first saw a young couple in marital and individual therapy. The wife requested that I see her and her brother, then they wished to include their sister. The three of them requested special family therapy sessions to include their parents and, eventually their grandmother joined us. The couple returned several years later when they were planning their family and, still later, after the birth of their children. We had moved all the way up and down the generation ladder.

I enjoyed working with families that included children and adolescents. Sometimes I found the youngsters related to me as if I were a kindly grandmother instead of another parental authority. My chronological age difference made it easier for me to move in and out of the family system as needed, and to maintain a distance from the family conflict that was more comfortable for me and allowed for more effective treatment.

Some of the families I saw returned for therapy at different stages of the family's development. I saw one family when their children were in grammar school and again when they were in high school. The parents returned in their midlife crisis. One of their daughters requested a family interview before her marriage, not wanting to repeat some of the conflicts she knew had existed in her family.

Working with families of adolescents, confronted with the decision of whether to keep their infants or relinquish them for adoption, reminded me of my child welfare days. I caught up with changes in adoption laws, practices, life styles, attitudes, only to realize that the feelings of natural parents and adoptive parents had hardly changed at all in fifty years.

Seeing Japanese-American families, who had been interned in World War II, reminded me of families I had known at Langley Porter and Berkeley Mental Health. Those families had never been able to tell their children of their shame at being interned by their own country. In the 60s, one such family had gone so far as to physically restrain their daughter, a student, so that she would not participate in the Free Speech Movement; they feared she might be incarcerated and held in jail. And now I saw in the next generation, the problems engendered by keeping that terrible event secret.

Families who lost their homes in the firestorm in the Oakland and Berkeley hills in 1991 required me to use all I knew about crisis intervention and tapped my counter-transference. I had experienced my family's loss of their home by fire when I was in my twenties, and found I had not fully come to terms with the impact of that trauma on my life.

In focusing on work with the aging, I found my efforts to raise consciousness about the aging process were not always well-received, either in my professional community or in the community at large. I was reminded of earlier experiences in which my interest in social work was not acceptable as dinner table conversation, and people moved away when they learned I was a psychotherapist, as if I could read their minds. Even though the increase in the aging population was an accepted fact, my efforts in social situations were often frowned upon. I was shocked at how few of my colleagues were willing to see patients who were on Medicare.

My perspective on the subject of aging was broadened by leading workshops, attending conferences held by the Western Society On Aging and the National Scientific Conference on Geriatrics. But it was the women in my over-60 psychotherapy groups that opened my eyes when they talked about "being" themselves after lifetimes of "doing." I saw that I was experiencing my own transformation in the aging process.

◉ ◉ ◉ ◉ ◉

Balancing my time for my work and for my personal life provided an opportunity for a fuller life. Yoga, meditation, painting, walking my dogs in the Berkeley Hills and meeting my neighbors opened new doors for me. My husband was employed again in private industry. The return from an investment provided us a financial margin. We enjoyed the San Francisco Symphony and the Berkeley Repertory Theatre, joined a swim and country club, took our first trip to Europe for five weeks.

Bob and I enjoyed our land and cabin in the Sierra foothills. It had great meaning for both of us as we had bought it and worked on it together, dragging brush, moving rocks, and cutting trees. It reminded us of our early life experiences living in the country. Once again, we were without modern conveniences and enjoyed a wood stove and lamplight. We liked listening to country sounds and entertaining our friends there. We started developing our site for building the house we had designed by an architect. We were looking forward to making our home there.

My subconscious was activated as I dug into the adobe soil, while cleaning out the spring flowing with water beside a rock outcropping that still had grinding holes left by Maidu Indians. I found I had to dig deep into the soil of my life as well. In my reminiscences and life review I confronted the shadow and encountered my "self." My reawakened subconscious required active self-analysis. Recapturing and reorganizing memories to make sense became a preoccupation. Where had I gotten off track in my early relationships? What injury had I caused to others while finding my way? What really mattered? I found that I needed to reexamine my whole early childhood, and later development in the context of readings I was doing in professional study groups.

Confronting my anger, as a part of the real me, was not easy to deal with. My new self, without its wrappings, was not easy for others to deal with either, and required working out a new balance in my marriage and family life. I sometimes let loose at my safest targets—my husband, my mother, and my brother. Bob still kids me about an incident, in the Tuillieries Park, the first day we arrived in Paris. The preparation for our first trip to Europe had been an emotional and draining experience. In an ugly scene, in which I threatened to proceed for the rest of the journey alone, Bob reminded me that I might have trouble without my passport, which he carried safely in his belt.

A recurrence of feelings I should have dealt with long before emerged in my relationship with my mother. My attitudes were distressing and puzzling for her. I saw it as crucial that we relate to one another, as two adult women, with open discussions of our feelings and life-long experiences with each other. She didn't know what I was talking about. When I pressed her to acknowledge that she had a major part in seeing to it that I got out of the Orlean community, she admitted that she felt there was a better life out in the world for me than the farm life in our rural community. She said she had not realized I would go so far though. "Where did you think I would go?" I asked her. "Oh, maybe Richmond or Washington, but I never dreamed that you would go to California." That discussion led to reconciliation between us, to my compassion for her aloneness, and a closer relationship between us for the rest of her life. Finding my own voice had led me from anger to forgiveness.

Facing my childlessness was painful. Not having children was the biggest sorrow of my life. Feeling close to my roots, I realized that since my brother and I had no children, we were the last of our family line. But out of that came a resurgence of my generativity and wanting to leave the story of my life and work for social workers of the next century.

A new round of losses in my sixties meant I was beginning to know more personally about the inevitable losses of aging. The deaths of family members, friends, and contem-

poraries came rapidly. Our loss in a major financial investment required that we give up our dream of building a house
in the country and start from scratch in saving for our retirement. Bob lost his job with a one-day notice. Both of us were
confronted with life-threatening illnesses. For a while, we
had no medical insurance as medical and dental expenses
began to climb.

But as I became more in touch with my inner life, I experienced a re-birth. One of my powerful spiritual experiences
in my sixties was our visit to the sanctuary of Asclepios in
Greece, where long ago people pilgrimaged for healing. They
brought facsimiles of their diseased or damaged body parts,
exercised according to instruction, bathed in healing springs,
and descended into deep sleep and their subconscious. Often,
they awakened reporting miraculous dreams and were healed.
Learning of the faith of these people inspired me to re-think
the whole process of healing in psychotherapy and in life—
how to put the shattered pieces together. Other spiritual
experiences followed in the solitude I found in the Sierra
foothills, in Maine, in Virginia, in the Berkeley hills, and in
spiritual retreats.

And the privilege of being with my mother during her last
illness and death in Virginia was profoundly meaningful as I
reviewed her life and mine. I was grateful for the effort each of
us had made in later life to resolve the conflict in our earlier
relationship. As a woman of the twentieth century, she had
provided me a model for every phase of my adult development, and now she was a model for dying. The effect of my
early trauma about death was healed as I realized life and death
are a continuum. Observing the place she had found for herself in living independently in her rural community helped me
again to feel a part of that community. Her devoted friends
included me as they had included her. The overall experience
inspired me to find a place in my own community in Berkeley.

When I faced my disappointment that I would never live
in the country again, that I had no alternative, that Berkeley

was my home, I began to appreciate it more than ever before. Bob and I remodeled our kitchen and I enjoyed the domesticity I had so long delayed. We began to give more of our time and attention to making our home comfortable and to entertaining others. We enjoyed gardening together, took watercolor classes, attended Elder Hostel Workshops, and continued to enjoy our place in the country.

We became active in the Northbrae Community Church, a nondenominational church, where I have led groups and workshops, usually having to do to with creativity, aging, or the family. We worked in Christmas in April, a project which rehabilitates homes for the aging and disabled, and in the Community Cares Bank, where one of my favorite projects was taking junior high school students to visit a woman who suffered with Alzheimer's disease. We joined several book clubs, and a writers group. One of my book clubs, the Glorias, named after Gloria Steinem, had beautiful luncheons in our homes, a luxury I never had time for before. We made new friends and spent time with old friends.

Solano Avenue, Walnut Square, Rockridge, and, 4th Street were attractions for me as for others to "hang out." My friend and cousin, Joan, who visits us often from Virginia, asked, "Tell me Merle, why do people in Berkeley always have something in their hand to eat or drink?" "The bakeries and the cappuccino, I guess, Joan."

Our daughter got married in a big wedding and several years later we became grandparents. Grandparenting became one of the most satisfying experiences of my life. Bob and I take care of Geoffrey, age six, and Heidi three, in their home for a whole day every other week. Watching their development since infancy and our interactions with them are the highlights of our lives.

Our times together as a whole family are infrequent, as our son and our daughter and her husband who live in the San Francisco Bay area are busy professionals. But we enjoy celebrating birthdays, holidays, and special occasions together.

And right on target, as predicted by the adult development experts, Bob and I are experiencing one of the most companionable and harmonious times of our relationship. Time passes faster. We have more fun. If we feel like curling up in our window seat for a nap in the sun we do so.

In 1996, I carefully thought out my plan for retirement from my private practice. In March of that year, young friends from our church, Henry and Linda Lew Van Brocklin, gave me a retirement party attended by family, friends, and colleagues. My husband planned a trip to England, Ireland, and Scotland for us. Friends and family often inquired about my progress toward retirement. I knew I was dragging my heels, but I found good rationalizations for keeping the doors of my office open until the last day of that year.

The reasons I retired were, for me, sound, reasonable, acceptable intellectually. I had done enough. I wanted time for myself. I wanted to paint while I could still see, and due to cataracts, my vision was failing. I wanted to enjoy my family, friends, community, and living with the energy I had left in my seventies.

There was just one factor I had not anticipated. It was not the loss of my work, per se, but the loss of all that the person sitting across from me represented in my search for the ultimate connection with another human being.

Chapter 13:

PALIMPSEST AND PINK PILLOWS

In telling the story of my life and work, two images came to mind, both time worn and durable—palimpsest and pink pillows.

Palimpsest is defined as a written document, typically on vellum or parchment, that has been written upon several times, often with remnants of earlier, imperfectly erased writing still visible. (Lat: *palimpsestus*< GK, *palimsestos*, scraped again: *palin*, again+*psen*, to scrape)

I have laid down the layers of my experience as a social worker in the twentieth century, which I hope will be dusted off, scraped through, and, again, used in the next century.

Pink pillows line my white leather sofas in my home in Berkeley. I made them from a faded homespun counterpane. My great grandmother, Angeline Brown Updike, carded, spun, and wove the cloth used to make the bed coverlet, in the Shenandoah Valley of Virginia, in the century before I was born. The course of my life and work is certainly no less complex than the design of that homespun.

In September, 1997, a year after I retired from my private practice, by which time I was well into writing this book, I went back to Virginia to visit my brother and to retrace my footprints in my early life and work there. More than a half century had passed since I heard the call to social work in the Fauquier County Welfare Department. My search for footprints took me into the reaches of my inner being.

The sand and clay roads I remembered were hard-surfaced roads that led to places I did not recall. The scenery had changed. The old farms I once knew had become vineyards or real estate developments of small ten-acre farms. The one-room Wheatley school where my mother taught in the twenties had long since been demolished. Hume and Marshall High Schools, I attended in the thirties, had burned down. I could not remember what road led to the old farmhouse where my childhood sweetheart, Harfield Brown, lived, and settled for finding his grave in the Leeds' churchyard. For the first time, I exchanged my memory of the ruddy-cheeked boy for the reality of the lichen-covered gravestone that marked his fall at Anzio Beach in 1944.

My arrival for my visit at my brother's home on our family home place was timed perfectly for me to support him in his opposition to a proposal for hard surfacing the country road that ran through the middle of his farm. Once this road had gates to separate the fields from one another. He took me to a public hearing of the Fauquier County Board of Supervisors' Road Committee.

One of my brother's neighbors passed around photographs of the 200-year-old trees that would need to be destroyed in order to widen the road for hard surfacing. I realized that the old oak tree in front of the house where I was born was in jeopardy. I felt as if I would lay down my life to protect that old tree. It provided shade for my childhood tea parties and for my father and his threshing farmhands to rest at noon when they came in for dinner. I felt as fiercely independent, as self-consciously isolated, and as loyal to family as a mountaineer to her clan. Where had that fierce independence come from?

A book I read at my brother's was illuminating. *Our Southern Highlanders: A Narrative of Adventure in the Southern Appalachians As A Study of Life Among The Mountaineers* by Horace Kephart, an amateur anthropologist and friend of the family, was written in 1923, the year I was born. The mountaineers are described as set apart by dialect, customs, and by self-conscious isolation.

Kephart traces the origin of the mountaineers to the Scotch-Irish who settled the southern Appalachians. "To be free, unbeholden is a part of the fiery individualism of the Scotch-Irish mountaineers....Every person is accorded the consideration that his own qualities entitle him to, no wit more," is a quote from Kephart that might well have been a quote from my father.

Ancestors on both sides of my family had lived in or at the base of that Appalachian range and had intermarried with Scotch-Irish settlers. It seemed to me that the Dutch, English, German, and Scotch-Irish strains of my ancestry blended into the Blue Ridge mountaineer. Finding Kephart's book, and my baseline identity as a mountaineer, solved a lot of questions about my romanticizing of isolation, my longing for others. My spirit was fired with re-discovery.

Fierce individualism is one of the character traits Kephart attributes to the Appalachian mountaineer. I knew that it came down from my families of origin. As lonely as it made me as a child, as masqued by passivity as it became in my early adulthood, as obstructive as it was in my thirties in my autonomous thrust toward independence, as the rudder it provided me in reclaiming a life of my own and preserving my professional identity, this individualism provided a ballast through it all.

Another book I found at my brother's home led me on a serendipitous pilgrimage to the Fort Valley that made more of the connections clear. *The History of the Halterman, Ross,*

O'Flaherty and Cullers Families in Powell's Fort Valley had caught my attention when my mother, whose maiden name was Cullers, was alive. But when I looked at it this time, I found, in the book, an empty envelope addressed in my mother's handwriting to Maizie Cullers, Fort Valley Road, R.F.D., Fort Valley, Virginia. I remembered that I had heard her name before. I did not know the exact connection, but I had many times heard the story of my great grandfather Eli Cullers crossing the Massanutten Mountains from the Fort Valley to marry my great grandmother Arthelia Wood, and bring up his family on a farm by the Shenandoah River. My husband and my brother joined me for a trip to the Fort Valley "over the mountain" as my parents would say, and "out back of beyond" as Kephart would describe it.

The Fort Valley is on the other side of the Massanutten Mountains from Bentonville, the village in the Shenandoah Valley where my parents were brought up. It stretches from Strasburg to Luray and is bounded by the Massanutten Mountains on one side and a mountain range of the Alleghenies on the other. Quiet, clean, small farms with meadows and hayfields; simple homes; churches; cemeteries. No fast food chains, no real estate developments, no gas filling stations. Only one country store where we learned, "Maizie Cullers lives just down the road and can tell you anything you want to know about the Fort Valley."

Maizie, a distant relative whom I had never met before, grabbed her broad-brimmed straw hat, offered to show us around, and captivated us with stories of her people and mine. She gave us a tour of the Fort Valley Museum, to which she had the only key. It contained old Bibles, costumes, Civil War memorabilia, flags, and farm instruments. She showed us churches and cemeteries, the remains of the Seven Fountains, once healing springs, now a beautiful lake reflecting the autumn colors of the mountains. Then she suggested that we might want to climb down over the hill to see the grave of John Cullers, my great, great, great grandfather, who was born in 1747, according to the marking on his simple gravestone. Maizie was saddened by the thought of the Cullers' home place going out of the hands of the family; she suggested we might want to see it as it was for sale and open to the public on that day.

The land belonged to John Cullers in 1777. The farm and homestead looked much as it might have at the end of the eighteenth century—an old frame and log house on a stone foundation, neatly kept barns, and out buildings, a small stream with a footbridge. I would have bought it on the spot if I had had the money.

I found myself crossing the stream on the footbridge made of split oak logs with flat boards nailed on top for a walkway, and a small wooden fence serving as a handrail on either side of the bridge. Approached on one side from a bed of sand and pebbles glistening in the sun, the bridge led to deep shade from a cluster of trees on the other side.

As I looked into that dark mirror of the stream, reflecting my life back to me, the chronological form disappeared. Sequential segments contrasted and compared, juxtaposed and overlapped, contracted and expanded before my eyes. In the swirl of time, past, present, and future became one. I saw a dynamic mix of light and shadow, of the oscillations of inside and outside, conscious and unconscious, self and other, individual and society.

When I contemplated what held it all together, I knew that the historical, personal, and professional lines were inter-woven. These lines sometimes ran a parallel course, sometimes crossed, often intertwined. The complexity of my life as a social worker was matched by that of my identity as a woman of the twentieth century.

I thought of my pink pillows. Historians of Appalachian weaving tell me that the basic pattern of the homespun is "Overshot," that my great grand mother, Angie evidently wove her unique design into that basic pattern.

The overshot connects and decorates the warp and the weft.

The lines of my personal and professional experience, woven in and out of the time blocs of my life, seemed as sturdy as the warp and the weft of that faded homespun. The brilliance of my life blood had faded just as the brilliant deep red from plant dyes in the pink pillows had faded, but the design was unmistakably my own. I thought of the connections that had been so important in my life and how they flowed through each segment, intertwining and connecting, to form the pattern.

My connection to place was strong throughout my life. A few years ago, in an art class, I made a self-portrait collage from different stages of my life. My favorite places furnished the back drop—the Shenandoah Valley, Fauquier County, New York City, San Francisco, Berkeley, and the Sierra Nevada foothills, which looked surprisingly like the foothills of the Blue Ridge Mountains of Virginia. That connection with place went back to my idyllic childhood. I thought of Geoffrey, our grandson who, at the age of four, along with his family, was preparing for a move to a new house. When asked what he would take with him, he squared his shoulders and proudly announced, "My tree and my grass."

My childhood search for connection with others sent me on a lifelong search for community. In adolescence and youth, I sought diversity and depth in friendships. Finding the balance between distance and intimacy was difficult and took me on some painful detours. But in every stage of my life, I made a few close friends and most of them became lifelong friends. In mid-life, I confronted my regret that I had not given more of myself in those cherished relationships. As I grew older, I found my friendships deepened and expanded.

I thought of connection with self as beginning at the outset of life and running to the end. It develops throughout childhood, adolescence, and adulthood, and, at some point, we shed the shell for the emergence of the real self. My experience in psychoanalytic treatment and my experience in marriage were the two relationships in which I learned to be most completely and authentically myself. But it was not until late life, when the shell was shed, that I felt truly comfortable with myself. By then, some of the opposite pulls, the yin and the yang, were sufficiently brought into balance that I could live with them. The effort to balance those opposites continues as long as we live.

The need for self-awareness in the therapeutic relationship was perhaps the greatest gift crossing over from my career to my self. To know one's strengths and limitations, to be in touch with one's conscious will and underlying motivation, requires continuous effort. Learning to trust one's intuition as well as one's judgment became a way of life for me.

If I were to name one reciprocal gift from my self to my work, it would be the gift of solitude, that precious space I learned early in life. To gather oneself in a quiet place is essential for the therapist in every therapy hour, in order to listen to the person across from him or her. It also becomes essential for self-replenishment between hours.

Connection with society took me full circle as I thought of the state of the world and of our responsibility. I sometimes wonder if the last thing I do in life will be to write one more letter to a legislator.

And when I thought of the connection with whatever it is that is larger and longer lasting than any of us, I thought of those old-fashioned values that sustain us: faith as a quality of living that helps us to find meaning in the universe and in our own lives, and hope that enables us to face whatever is before us with conviction.